CW00547327

Fishing with Emma

HOW TO FISH FOR:

Carp, Roach, Rudd, Barbel
Perch, Chub, Zander, Bream
Catfish, Dace, Tench and Pike

David Overland

Merlin Unwin Books

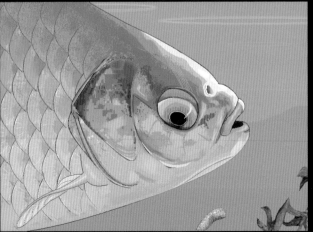

First published in Great Britain by Merlin Unwin Books, 2013

Text and illustrations © David Overland, 2013

Published by:

Merlin Unwin Books Ltd
Palmers House
7 Corve Street
Ludlow
Shropshire SY8 1DB U.K.

www.merlinunwin.co.uk

The author asserts his moral right to be identified with this work.

Designed and set in Comic Sans by David Overland.

Printed by Great Wall Printing.

ISBN 978-1-906122-50-8

**For Dad who taught me to fish
and taught me to paint**

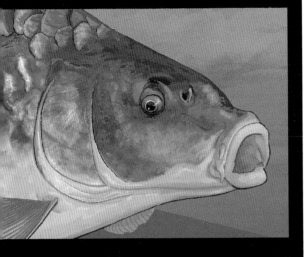

Contents

About the Author

David Overland was born in Newport, Wales, in 1960 and throughout his working life as a civil servant, for the charity sector and later in the ornamental fish industry, he's also worked as a Freelance Illustrator, writing and drawing comics, book illustrations and record covers.

David lives in Monmouthshire with his wife Mary and their two sons, Sam and Ben. He has been a passionate coarse fisher all his life.

Foreword

As a child I spent many happy hours fishing with my Grandfather on the banks of the Norfolk Broads. He was a man of few words and so I watched what he did and copied him, putting on worms, maggots or small lumps of bread. Things were simple in those days, nothing more than a rod and a few floats. We caught roach, perch and other types of small fish, with rarely a blank day.

Later when my sons were small, I in turn took them fishing and passed on the knowledge I had gained from my Grandfather. But I wasn't able to explain why we did things like we did; I had never been told, I had just copied Grandad. If only *Fishing with Emma* had been published then. It explains all the different techniques for catching the main species of coarse fish – and why they work.

Fishing with Emma has great appeal for everyone: young and old, beginners and experienced hands, men and women alike. In fact, everyone who has an interest in angling will both enjoy and benefit from Emma's words of wisdom. It is easy to read, informative and entertaining: the pictures are delightful.

I wasn't certain that I liked Emma at first – I think I was jealous of the tight jeans! However, as I looked through the pages I became more keen to see what she was up to next, and what she was going to catch, and how she was going to do it.

As for me, I have recently acquired a small stream of my own and I am able to spend a few contemplative hours fishing quietly, just as I did when I was young. But now, having read this book, I will know exactly what I am doing and why, I hope, the dace will be there waiting for me!

– *Sally Pizii, Angling Coach*

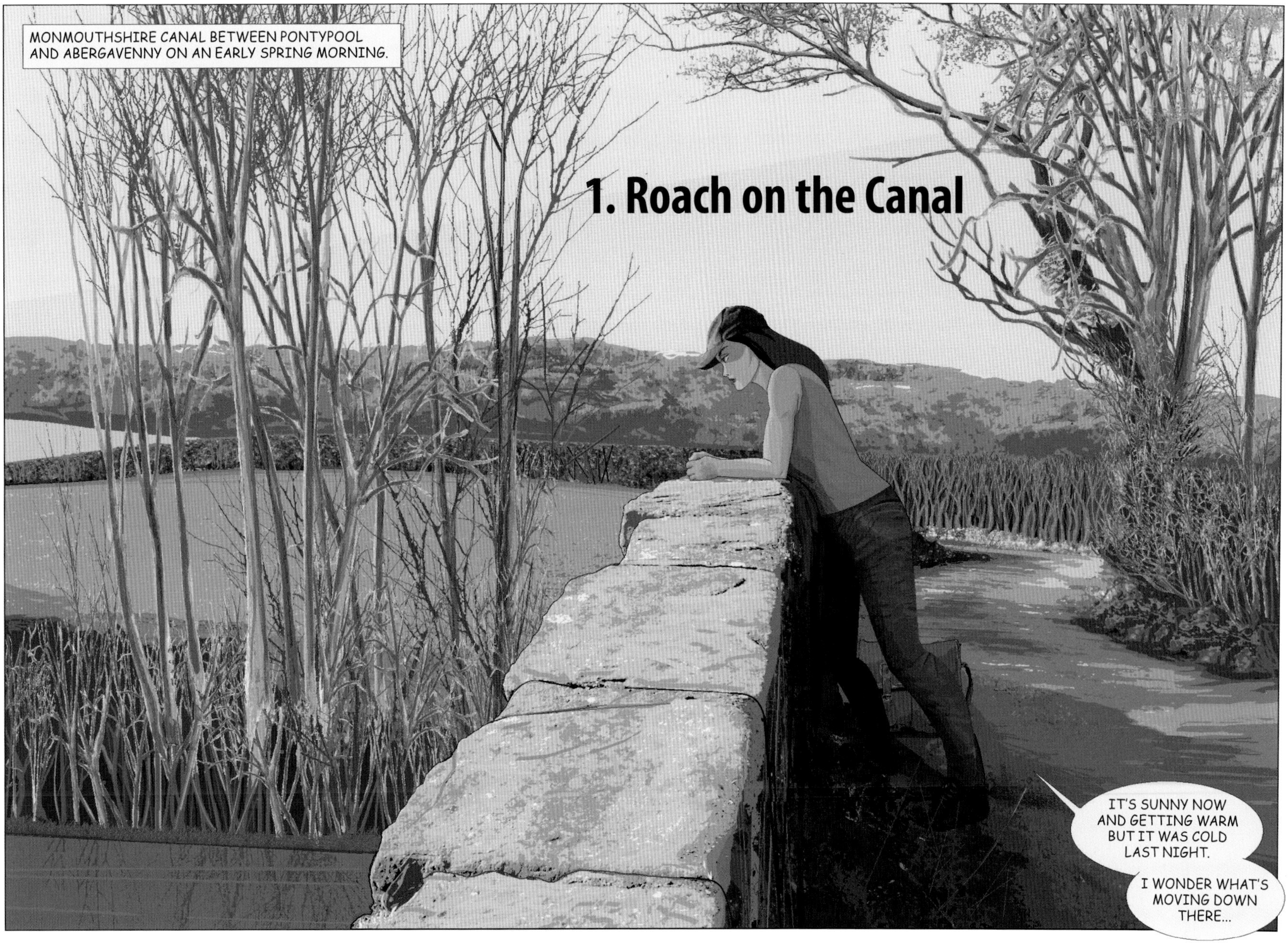
MONMOUTHSHIRE CANAL BETWEEN PONTYPOOL AND ABERGAVENNY ON AN EARLY SPRING MORNING.
1. Roach on the Canal
IT'S SUNNY NOW AND GETTING WARM BUT IT WAS COLD LAST NIGHT.
I WONDER WHAT'S MOVING DOWN THERE...

LET'S SEE...

THIS SPOT HAS OVERHANGING TREES ON THE FAR BANK

AND A BRIDGE TO MY RIGHT

FISH ARE DRAWN TO STRUCTURE AND COVER

BRIDGES PROVIDE BOTH – SO ARE A GOOD STARTING POINT

OVERHANGING TREES ARE ANOTHER FISH MAGNET

EARLIER I THREW SOME BALLS OF GROUNDBAIT INTO THE SWIM FROM THE BRIDGE

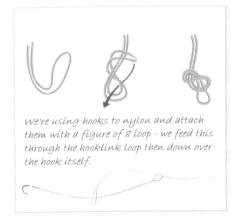

We're using hooks to nylon and attach them with a figure of 8 loop - we feed this through the hooklink loop then down over the hook itself.

Emma's first decision is where to fish. Cover from the bridge and the trees on the far bank provide an excellent holding spot for fish. As well as shelter and cover, later in the year berries and insects will fall from the trees making them a superb larder. Although it's early in the year and they've no leaves yet, there will still be fish hanging around under them.

Most canals have a shallow shelf either side of a deeper middle channel, so the first job is to work out the depth. Emma's fished here many times and knows the depth, contours and layout beneath the surface, so she doesn't need to do this (but check out the chapter on Crucian Carp where she'll show you how this is done).

Throughout the book Emma's using cheap basic tackle to demonstrate that you don't need to spend too much to get started in fishing. Her rod today is an 11-foot Match rod (basically a float rod) which is ideal for this sort of fishing. The rod is an entry level rod from one of the main tackle manufacturers which she bought with the reel for around £30.

She's prepared her swim with Groundbait. This powder, when mixed with water, attracts fish into the area and gets them looking around for food.

Emma added some breadcrumb and maggots to the mix and has brought maggots and a small tub of worms along for bait.

Her line is 4lb (0.14 dia) breaking strain and she's using a size 18 barbless hook on a short 2lb (0.08 dia) hooklink. The weaker line is hookside to protect the fish. If the line does break it'll break at its weakest point on the hooklink, well below the float, so a fish won't be left dragging the float and shot around with it.

The Waggler is a float that's perfect for stillwater. It is attached bottom-end only and locked into place with the bulk of the shot.

Splitshot are tiny round weights that can be squeezed onto the line, tight enough to hold their position but not too tight that they can't be reopened with a fingernail and moved.

This Float takes 4AAAs, so Emma uses 3AAAs and a BB to lock the float and then six No. 8s go on to the lower half of the line. So if there's 4 feet of line below the float then the smaller shot are evenly spaced on the lower 2 feet of line.

This is all about casting – splitting the weights in this way will keep the hook and the float apart as they're cast.

Shot	Weight	
SSG	1.6g	2XAAA
AAA	0.8g	2XBB
BB	0.4g	2XNo4
No1	0.3g	3XNo6
No3	0.25g	2XNo6
No4	0.2g	3XNo9
No5	0.15g	2XNo8
No6	0.1g	2XNo10
No8	0.06g	2XNo11
No9	0.05g	
No10	0.04g	2XNo12
No11	0.08g	
No12	0.02g	2XNo13
No13	0.01g	

THE BEST WAY TO HOOK A MAGGOT IS TO NICK THE POINT OF THE HOOK THROUGH THE LOOSE SKIN AROUND THE TWO DARK SPOTS (BREATHING TUBES) ON THE BLUNT END - THIS WAY THEY'LL LOOK NATURAL AND STAY WRIGGLING LONGER.

OUR RIG IS SIMPLE –

A WAGGLER

A FEW SHOT AND THE HOOKLINK

THE BULK OF THE WEIGHT OF SHOT LOCK THE FLOAT

THE REMAINDER ARE EVENLY SPACED ALONG THE BOTTOM HALF OF THE LINE UNDER THE FLOAT

LIKE THIS

NOW WE CAN CAST TO THOSE REEDS –

TREE ROOTS

OR SHOWING FISH

THOSE BUBBLES ARE FISH ON TO OUR GROUNDBAIT –

SO I'LL JUST FLICK THE FLOAT –

RIGHT INTO THE MIDDLE OF THEM

NOW EMMA CAN'T SEE WHAT'S HAPPENING UNDER THE SURFACE BUT LOOK HOW EASY IT IS FOR US.

THERE ARE THREE MAIN SPECIES THAT THE ANGLER MIGHT COME ACROSS ON THIS PARTICULAR STRETCH OF CANAL –

SKIMMER BREAM

PERCH

AND ROACH

AND IT'S ROACH THAT ARE EMMA'S TARGET SPECIES FOR TODAY.

The trick to casting well is practice – do this with just the float and the shot and practice wherever and whenever you can. Practice distance, practice accuracy, try different shotting patterns, try different types of float, practice!

It's a given that fish will seek shelter and cover; it's another matter to be able to confidently cast your rig up to, rather than into, obstacles and avoid snagging up. So: practice.

Emma's using maggot on a size 18. Now this may seem a small hook but this is a lightly-fished canal. On some of the really hard-fished ones, you'd need to go even smaller.

It takes a while to get used to hooking maggots like this so don't worry if yours aren't perfect. Some anglers deliberately hook them through the body saying that this releases their juices which draw the fish in.

There are three main species in this part of the Canal:

Skimmer (juvenile Bream), deep-bodied shoaling fish which are a favourite with Match anglers.

Perch – bold, striped predators – are Emma's favourite fish (or more specifically a big Perch is Emma's favourite fish) and there are Roach.

Roach are found everywhere: rivers, ponds, lakes and streams as well as canals. Roach are a favourite of many anglers. A fish of a pound is a good one, a two-pounder is a real specimen and anything over two and a half is a monster!

Like many of our Coarse species small Roach are much easier to catch than big Roach which are a real challenge and a great achievement.

Emma casts into the area which she Groundbaited earlier as it's already showing signs of the presence of feeding fish. As soon as her float settles she throws a handful of maggots at it and after a few moments her float slides away.

The first Roach is small and can be swung safely to hand. Emma keeps a small pair of forceps within reach for easily unhooking small fish like this and the tiny barbless hooks come out easily.

The next fish is a Skimmer but for the next hour or so after, it's Roach all the way.

Now lots of anglers get annoyed by the boats but you must remember that these boats bring with them an opportunity.

Emma's got to bring in her line anyway, then she moves the shot up under the float and swaps maggot for worm. As the boat chugs past, its engine churns up the water, pulling great clouds of mud from the bottom.

She flicks her bait into the wash from the engines where the worm will sink slowly and bounce around in all that stirred-up muddy water.

Remember that the fish are used to the boats and that the older fish, the wiser fish, the bigger fish, have realised that as the boat stirs up the bottom, all sorts of goodies get drawn up in the water.

Moving the shot away from the hook allows the bait to move naturally around in the churned-up water but it also makes the rig much harder to cast. This is where all that practice bears fruit. With all the shot

under the float, a tangle is much more likely. Casting with an upward underarm flick will prevent this (if you practice) or simply cast as normal but stop the line by dropping your finger onto the spool as the rig's about to hit the surface, which will straighten everything out as it lands.

Emma's trick finds a bigger Roach. Whether they follow the boats or whether the boats draw them out, she doesn't know but many of her best canal Roach have fallen to this method.

A soft rod with a full action is a rod that bends easily along its length. This allows the rod to act as a shock-absorber, especially useful with barbless hooks. Playing a fish is the process of tiring it out prior to netting. It's natural to want to see the fish especially if it's pulling back

a bit but trying to hurry a fish or get it to the surface too soon can cause real problems.

Emma uses her Landing net to get the fish out; she keeps the net out in front of her with one hand whilst drawing the fish over it with the rod in her other. It pays to practice this with smaller fish so that on the day you bag a monster, you'll know what you're doing.

Emma carries on fishing and soon swaps worm for Caster. She also fishes around the edges of the area where the fish are feeding as the larger fish are often suspicious and can hang back. She feeds regularly but sparingly and soon puts together a good catch of Roach. She doesn't usually use a keepnet but on this occasion it allows us to see the results.

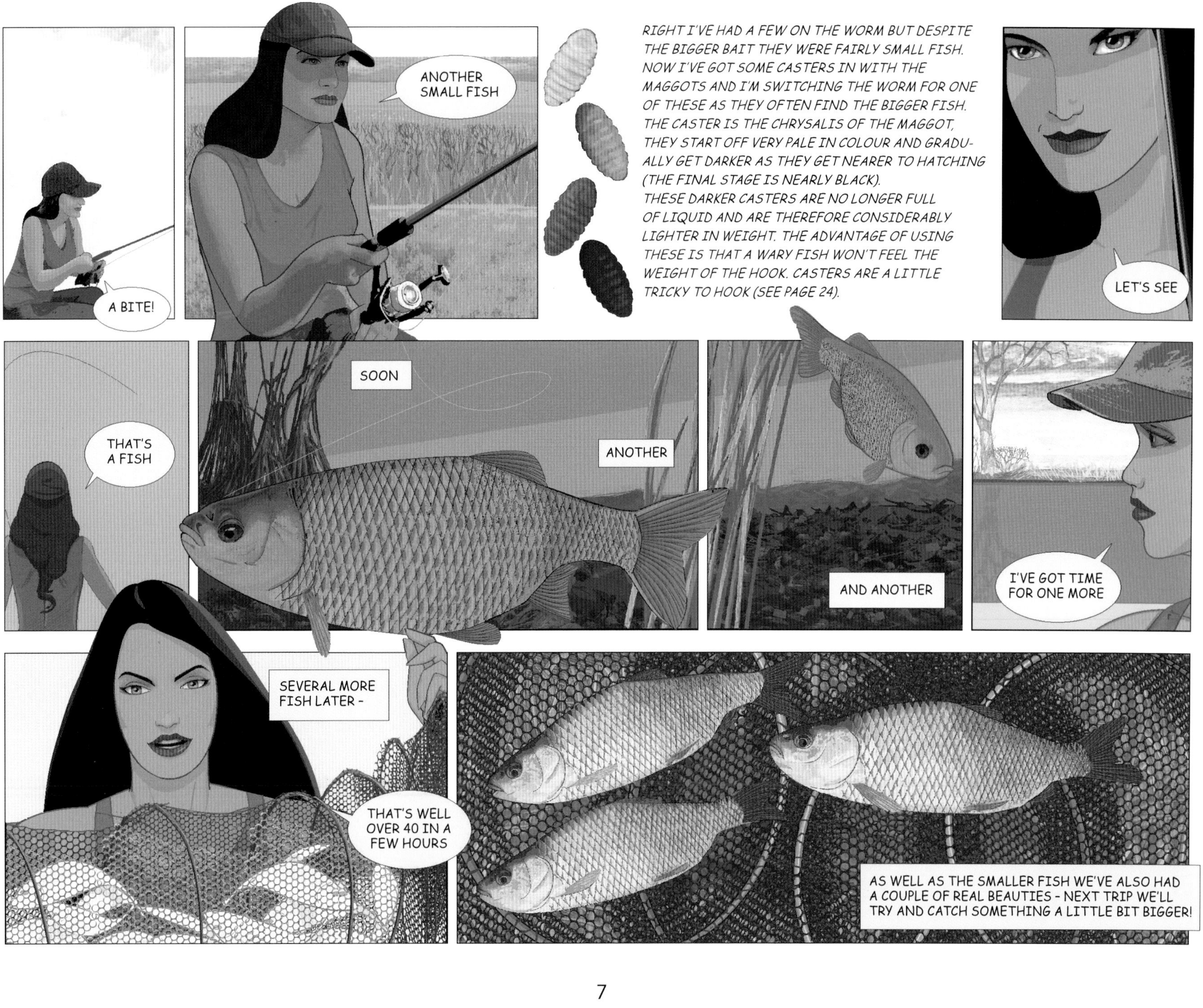

A BITE!
ANOTHER SMALL FISH
RIGHT I'VE HAD A FEW ON THE WORM BUT DESPITE THE BIGGER BAIT THEY WERE FAIRLY SMALL FISH. NOW I'VE GOT SOME CASTERS IN WITH THE MAGGOTS AND I'M SWITCHING THE WORM FOR ONE OF THESE AS THEY OFTEN FIND THE BIGGER FISH. THE CASTER IS THE CHRYSALIS OF THE MAGGOT, THEY START OFF VERY PALE IN COLOUR AND GRADUALLY GET DARKER AS THEY GET NEARER TO HATCHING (THE FINAL STAGE IS NEARLY BLACK). THESE DARKER CASTERS ARE NO LONGER FULL OF LIQUID AND ARE THEREFORE CONSIDERABLY LIGHTER IN WEIGHT. THE ADVANTAGE OF USING THESE IS THAT A WARY FISH WON'T FEEL THE WEIGHT OF THE HOOK. CASTERS ARE A LITTLE TRICKY TO HOOK (SEE PAGE 24).
LET'S SEE
THAT'S A FISH
SOON
ANOTHER
AND ANOTHER
I'VE GOT TIME FOR ONE MORE
SEVERAL MORE FISH LATER -
THAT'S WELL OVER 40 IN A FEW HOURS
AS WELL AS THE SMALLER FISH WE'VE ALSO HAD A COUPLE OF REAL BEAUTIES - NEXT TRIP WE'LL TRY AND CATCH SOMETHING A LITTLE BIT BIGGER!

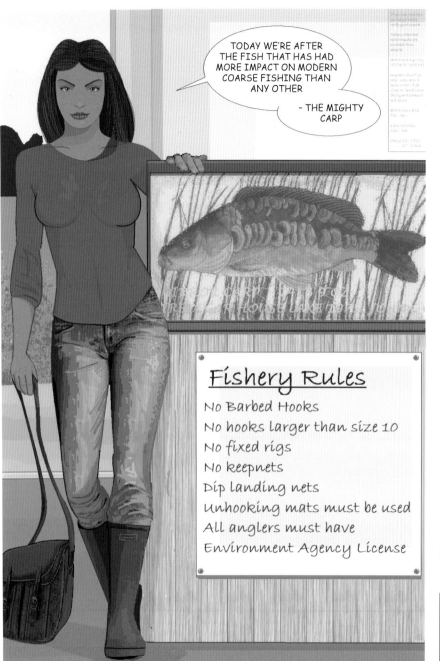

TODAY WE'RE AFTER THE FISH THAT HAS HAD MORE IMPACT ON MODERN COARSE FISHING THAN ANY OTHER

– THE MIGHTY CARP

Fishery Rules

No Barbed Hooks

No hooks larger than size 10

No fixed rigs

No keepnets

Dip landing nets

Unhooking mats must be used

All anglers must have

Environment Agency License

2. Carp from a Commercial Fishery

Fishing running legers and feeders

The Carp in the showcase is a reminder of a time when a 20lb Carp was considered a real Specimen.

A generation later, Carp have got huge. A 30lb Carp is now a real possibility and the British record is not far from 70lb.

Carp are far more accessible now. Commercial fisheries all over the country offer anglers the chance to take on these powerful, dogged fighters and today Emma has invited us along to see these fish for ourselves.

Although Legering may not have the appeal of Float fishing, it does allow the angler to fish at a much greater range and is an essential skill for today's angler.

Emma's also going to show us the Feeder, in this case a Maggot Feeder. This popular method allows the angler to present the bait surrounded by free samples. These samples draw the fish in and as they graze on them, sooner or later one of the fish will pick up the bait.

The setup Emma is using is Legering in its purest form. Later on she'll show us some more modern variations and additions to this classic technique.

Emma's encounters with Carp began in similar way to mine. When my Dad took me fishing as a kid we'd sometimes visit a farm outside

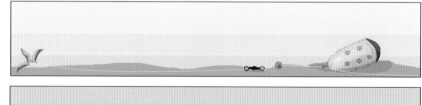

Chepstow, slip the farmer a fiver, then fish his pond for 'Wildies' (Wild Carp).

Nowadays things have moved on. Many farmers finding themselves squeezed financially in all directions started digging ponds into spare parcels of land and setting them up as fisheries. Entrepreneurs started buying up land to jump on the bandwaggon and in no time, Commercial fisheries were everywhere.

As more and more started up, competition between them increased and often higher and higher stocking levels were used to entice anglers. It worked and soon, many of them were giving up the rivers and canals to go and bag up at the local Commercial.

Now it's fair to say that there's many different opinions about stocked fisheries among anglers. At their worst, it's Fish in a Barrel, a large muddy puddle so full of starving fish that it's practically impossible not to catch.

At their best, they're lovely ponds and lakes in natural settings holding fair numbers of well-conditioned good-sized fish that are no push-over.

The truth is of course that they all vary and it's only those that are well managed and sensitively run that keep going.

Whether they like Commercials or not, most anglers would agree that there's no better place to learn how to handle bigger fish. If Emma had wanted a Carp from the canal she fished earlier, it would take time to find the right location and she'd probably need to pre-bait and she wouldn't even consider trying this early in the year.

NOW FOR OUR NEXT SPECIES WE'RE GOING TO TURN OUR ATTENTION TO CARP

AND USE A TECHNIQUE CALLED LEGERING

IT'S EARLY IN THE YEAR AND STILL COLD

AND THAT'S WHY WE'RE HERE

THIS IS A COMMERCIAL FISHERY AND COME SUMMER YOU CAN'T MOVE DOWN HERE

BUT TODAY WE'VE GOT THE POND AND THE CARP –

– TO OURSELVES

THE TWO MAIN TYPES OF CARP IN HERE ARE –

MIRROR

AND COMMON

THERE'S ONLY CARP IN THIS POND

MOST ARE SMALL . . .

BUT THERE ARE DECENT FISH IN HERE TOO

Today even though it's early March and cold, she'll catch Carp.

If you're learning, a place like this at a time like this is ideal. Get a good-sized Carp that runs you all over the pond and there's no other lines out there for you to worry about. We're also going to be fishing with two rods and it's better to get used to this method when it's quiet.

The Carp in this pond are the fully scaled 'Common' and the partially scaled 'Mirror'. Both are varieties of King Carp. The name Mirror Carp comes from the large irregular scales that appear on the fish's flanks. These fish were originally bred for food and a small number of large scales are easier to remove than hundreds of small ones.

Whenever you visit a Fishery for the first time, you need to check the rules. One of the rules here is no Fixed rigs.

Most rigs, Leger or Feeder, can be fished Running or Fixed.

With a Running rig the lead or Feeder is not tied to the line so that when a fish picks up the bait, the line just pulls through the eye of the swivel on the lead or the Feeder. The fish feels no resistance and on the bankside a Bobbin, Quivertip or Bite alarm signals the bite.

With a Fixed rig the lead or Feeder is tied directly to the line, usually only inches from the hook. The fish picks up the bait, feels the resistance of the weight and tries to spit out the bait but the downward pressure of the weight pulls the hook into its bottom lip. This type of rig is called a Bolt rig.

Emma's attaching the hooklink with a swivel. A sliding bead will prevent

OK, FIRST THINGS FIRST - LOCATION

THE FISH WILL OVERWINTER IN THE DEEPEST PART OF THE POND. ALTHOUGH IT'S SPRING NOW IT HASN'T WARMED UP THAT MUCH SO I DOUBT THAT THE FISH WILL HAVE MOVED TOO FAR

SO WE'LL POSITION OURSELVES IN FRONT OF THE DEEPER WATER

NOW WE'RE GOING TO FISH WITH TWO RODS

STRAIGHT RUNNING LEGER ON THE ONE

THE SECOND RIG IS THE SAME ONLY WITH A MAGGOT FEEDER INSTEAD OF THE LEAD.

I'M USING SWEETCORN WITH THE LEAD

AND A BUNCH OF MAGGOTS WITH THE FEEDER.

the eye of the Feeder/lead from jamming in it. The inset (page 10) shows a leger stop which is an alternative to using a swivel and bead.

The Maggot Feeder is a small tub full of holes that you fill with maggots. As soon as it sinks the maggots will start to wriggle out through these holes and draw fish toward your bait.

In waters where there are no silver fish present, maggots can be deadly.

Usually when fishing with a Feeder, it is common to repeatedly cast to the same spot every twenty minutes or so at the start of the session, to build up a carpet of food in the area that you're fishing. But as with the canal Emma knows that too much food when the water's cold is counter-productive. So she feeds both rigs sparingly.

Despite the presence of several large Carp in the pond, Emma isn't using a 'Carp' rod as such.

Carp fishing is one of the biggest and most popular branches of the sport and can involve catching huge fish at extreme range and modern Carp rods reflect this.

If Emma was fishing a gravel pit or large lake with a heavy Feeder and expecting really big fish then she'd opt for a proper Carp rod and big pit-style reel.

But this pond is barely two acres and although there's one or two 'Twenties' in here, the bulk of the fish are medium-to-high singles.

Despite this she's not going to use the rod that she used at the canal either.

THE DEEPER WATER IS AN EASY LOB FROM HERE

WHEN I CAST THE CORN IN – I KEPT MY EYES ON THE SPOT WHERE THE LEAD LANDED

THEN I CATAPULTED HALF A DOZEN FREEBIES INTO THE CENTRE OF THE SURFACE RINGS

YOU MUST BE CAREFUL NOT TO OVERFEED WHEN IT'S COLD

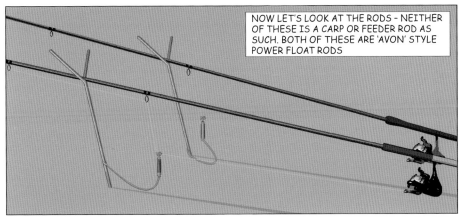

NOW LET'S LOOK AT THE RODS – NEITHER OF THESE IS A CARP OR FEEDER ROD AS SUCH. BOTH OF THESE ARE 'AVON' STYLE POWER FLOAT RODS

FISHED WITH BOBBINS FOR BITE INDICATION

AND NOW WE WAIT

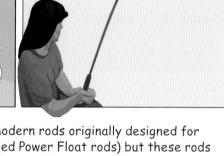

Even a medium-sized Carp on a very light Match rod is a real handful.

Carp are powerful fish and strong, dogged fighters. If the rod is too light then sometimes the fight can go on for too long and the fish can become exhausted. This is especially true in hot weather when the oxygen levels in the water are low.

The rods she's using fall between the two, stronger than a conventional Match/Float rod but not as heavy as a Carp rod.

She could have used Feeder rods and will do later when she really looks at Feeder fishing in-depth but today she's looking at Legering in its purest form.

Sometimes with modern tackle it can seem that you need to have a specific rod for each species and method but this simply isn't true.

The rods she's using today are modern rods originally designed for Pellet Waggler fishing (often called Power Float rods) but these rods are extremely versatile and can be used for many different styles of fishing and can cope with most species without difficulty.

For a new-comer with a limited budget, this type of rod is an excellent first choice. They have enough 'give' for smaller fish but enough 'grunt' to handle larger more powerful fish when they come along.

Emma's set her chair where she can easily reach both rods and with her landing net on her left. It pays to be as organised as possible on the bank especially when you're after larger fish like Carp. You'll notice also that (unlike many) she's not surrounded by tons of gear. She just takes what she's likely to need.

Handling a large fish out of water for the first time can be daunting and many find that a quiet fishery will make this a lot easier. If you're really unsure though, then it's probably better to fish with someone with experience. Carp can stand being out of water for longer than most fish but even so, you still need to get your fish unhooked then, if you wish, weighed and photographed as quickly as possible.

Firstly lay the fish, still in the net, onto a damp unhooking mat. If the fish is thrashing around, place your hand over its eye (this tends to calm them) then with your free hand remove the hook. Always keep a pair of forceps and a disgorger nearby. Carp have large mouths so it's usually fairly easy to get at the hook.

To pick the fish up, put one or two fingers into its mouth as Emma has.

Carp teeth are set right back in the throat so they don't bite. Place your other hand around the Anal fin as Emma has in the illustration, then lift it up against your chest. This becomes easier with practice; the key is confidence. If you handle a fish calmly and confidently the fish seem to sense this and they in turn seem more relaxed and less inclined to jump and thrash around.

If you want a photo, it's much safer if you're kneeling and as Emma has demonstrated, it won't show (especially if the photographer kneels as well).

The other important thing to remember when handling a fish out of water is to do it with wet hands which are a lot less likely to remove the fish's protective mucous (slime).

IT'S DACE THAT WE'RE AFTER TODAY – THEY'RE IN THE RIVER BUT WE CAN'T FISH THERE

3 Dace Chase
Trotting a small stream

Many angling books extol the virtues of fishing a river and it's true that running water brings its own unique set of problems and challenges. As well as their own species of fish, rivers seem to possess their own personality. Their changing moods and character can often make them a much more dynamic environment than stillwaters.

These books will urge the novice to get out and experience the delights of fishing a river for themselves but in many cases it's just not that simple.

Emma for example lives a few minutes away from the Usk and within easy reach of the Wye, both fabulous rivers teaming with fish but the most common bankside feature often seems to be signs bearing the words 'Private Fishing'.

One stretch of this bank is owned by one angling association, a different association has the fishing rights for the opposite bank for a few hundred yards, another group owns the next stretch and so on. It either costs a fortune to join one of these groups or they have waiting lists that run into years and nobody seems to know who owns what. At first sight, rivers seem to exist only for those who can afford to enjoy them but this isn't always true.

Visit the local tackle shop. They will know who owns what and which (if any) stretches are available to fish on a day ticket and what these stretches are like.

Don't ignore the streams that run into the main river. A chat with the landowner was all Emma needed today to get permission. Just because a stream may appear small or insignificant in comparison to the main river doesn't mean that there won't be fish in it. This is especially true if the main river is in flood.

BUT THIS FEEDER STREAM IS OURS FOR THE DAY – NOW IT MAY LOOK SMALL AND UNPROMISING

BUT THERE'S FISH HERE AND MORE THAN YOU MIGHT EXPECT

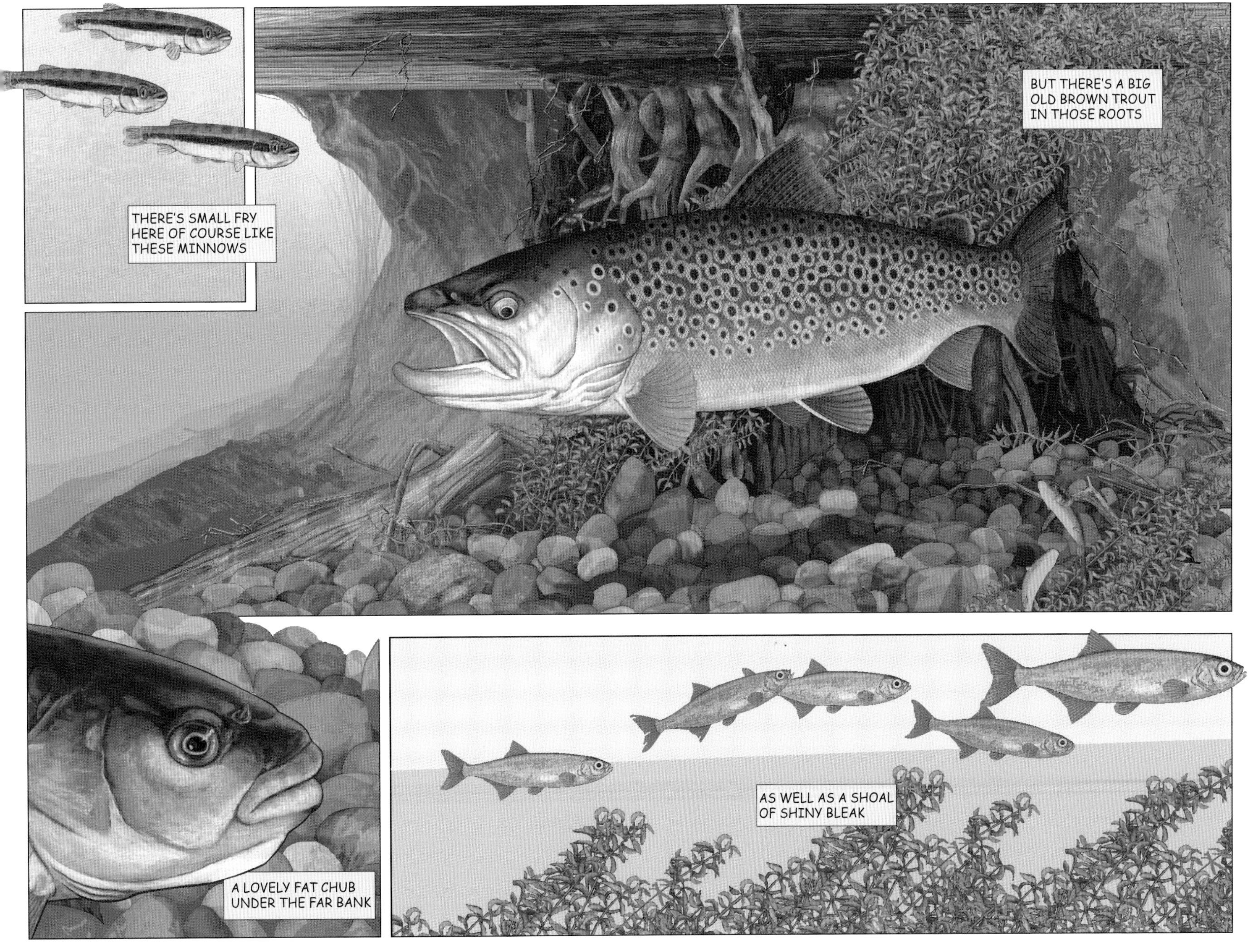
THERE'S SMALL FRY HERE OF COURSE LIKE THESE MINNOWS
BUT THERE'S A BIG OLD BROWN TROUT IN THOSE ROOTS
A LOVELY FAT CHUB UNDER THE FAR BANK
AS WELL AS A SHOAL OF SHINY BLEAK

As Emma starts to fish, we are able to take a look beneath the surface. We mentioned the different fish that can be found in rivers and that big Brown trout is one example. Trout are one of the reasons that some (usually upper) stretches of rivers can be so expensive to fish. Although obviously a Game fish and the usual quarry of flyfishermen, Trout themselves are frequently oblivious to the fact that they're only supposed to take flies and will enthusiastically grab and consume most baits that head in their direction. This is understandable when you're using maggot or worm perhaps but bread, cheesepaste and sweetcorn?! The fight of a Trout is as spectacular as its appearance and anglers who fish rivers will almost certainly come across one sooner or later.

Rather than using a catapult, today Emma's using an old maggot tub with holes drilled in the base. The constant drip of food will soon attract attention and allow Emma to concentrate on fishing rather than feeding.

Emma's going to use a method popular with river anglers called Trotting. This relies on the current to carry float and bait downstream. River fish spend most of their time swimming against the current waiting for food to be washed down to them. Trotting exploits this behaviour and allows the current to present the bait to the fish in a natural way. The line must be kept behind the float to ensure the bait moves realistically. It's very easy to get a bow in the line as the float trots downstream. This will drag the bait unnaturally across the current and prevent an effective strike. To 'mend' the line, raise the rod up and away from the float, gathering up the loose line of the bow until the line is straight to the float.

I'VE HUNG A TUB OF MAGGOTS UNDER A BUSH ON THE FAR BANK.

THERE ARE HOLES IN THE BASE OF THE TUB SO A SMALL STEADY STREAM OF MAGGOTS IS DROPPING INTO THE WATER.

THAT OLD TROUT SOON SPOTTED THEM

AND THE DACE WEREN'T FAR BEHIND HIM

THE MAGGOTS CREATE A TRAIL THAT THE FISH WILL FOLLOW

You can use a Waggler for Trotting but Emma's using the more traditional Stick float which is best cast underarm from one side. The shot are evenly spaced (shirt button style) No. 4 shot all the way down to a No. 6 nearest to the hook, which is a barbless 16 baited with maggot.

Emma's on the bank opposite the leaking tub of freebies and she wants the bait to match the speed and run of the maggots that are dropping in.

She casts across but leaves open the bale arm of the reel. By placing a finger across the spool she can control the speed that the line runs off.

Normally the float on the surface moves more quickly than the bait closer to the river bottom. That's because the stones that make up the bed of the stream slow the flow of the water down there. If Emma stops the float by placing her finger on the spool, the bait will continue moving until the line pulls tight, causing the bait to jerk up from the bottom. This sudden spurt of movement will often induce a bite.

Without doubt the best kind of reel for this type of fishing is a Centrepin but Emma's just demonstrating the basics today and a Fixed spool reel used in this way will get the job done.

When a bite comes, the finger is pressed against the spool, trapping the line as the rod is flicked into the strike. Then the moment you turn the reel handle the bale arm closes automatically and the hooked fish can be played as normal.

With Dace, all of this needs to be done very quickly as Dace are one of the fastest-biting of fish.

For this reason Dace are an excellent beginners' fish. If you can trot a small float down a river or stream and regularly hit Dace bites then there's nothing wrong with your reflexes or technique!

Emma catches many small Dace then decides to try and finish on a Chub. Her reason is to demonstrate the difference between the two. Both Dace and Chub are members of the family *Leuciscus* (as incidentally is the Orfe/Ide) and a small Chub is often mistaken for a big Dace.

She finds several Chub feeding further upstream but they ignore her maggots. The fish are greedily feeding on a hatch of flies and don't have eyes for anything else.

Emma resorts to an old trick that neatly brings together Coarse and Game fishing. A Black Gnat fly is combined with a small weighted float.

The float is attached top   end only with a band.

The float is there to provide casting weight and to enable you to see where the fly is, rather than just for bite indication.

When fishing this way you need to watch the fly carefully and strike the second it is hit rather than waiting for the float to move.

Emma watches her fly and soon has a Chub. Then she always wants another cast, and she gets another, then a third and then finally a big Dace.

Now a 12oz fish may not seem that big, but for a little stream like this, a Dace like that is a real specimen.

The Dace record is a little over a pound and a quarter.

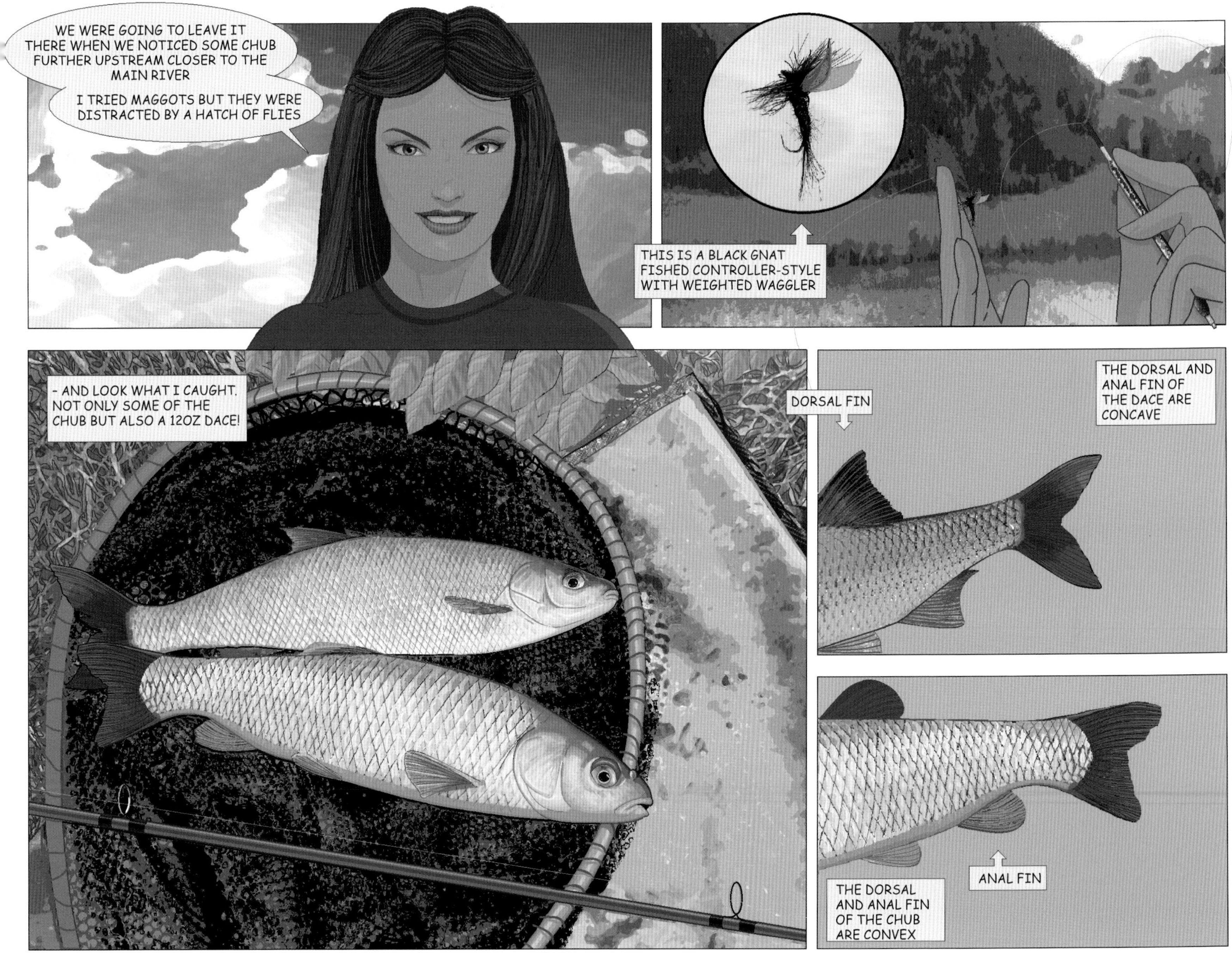
WE WERE GOING TO LEAVE IT THERE WHEN WE NOTICED SOME CHUB FURTHER UPSTREAM CLOSER TO THE MAIN RIVER
I TRIED MAGGOTS BUT THEY WERE DISTRACTED BY A HATCH OF FLIES
THIS IS A BLACK GNAT FISHED CONTROLLER-STYLE WITH WEIGHTED WAGGLER
- AND LOOK WHAT I CAUGHT. NOT ONLY SOME OF THE CHUB BUT ALSO A 12OZ DACE!
DORSAL FIN
THE DORSAL AND ANAL FIN OF THE DACE ARE CONCAVE
ANAL FIN
THE DORSAL AND ANAL FIN OF THE CHUB ARE CONVEX

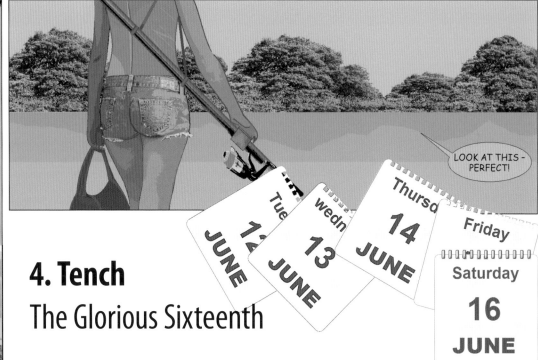

4. Tench
The Glorious Sixteenth

The Close season for Coarse fishing applies from March 15 to June 15. Nowadays it applies to all rivers, streams and drains in England and Wales but it used to cover stillwaters as well. Most lakes, ponds and canals no longer have a Close season (but there are one or two exceptions such as some Sites of Special Scientific Interest, if in doubt check the Environment Agency website). Many anglers remember when the Close season covered all waters and they know the excitement of the first day's fishing of the new season. Some would even camp out overnight on the 15th to fish at midnight or the following dawn and the species that became synonymous with the start of the season was the Tench.

Tench are fabulous fish. The colour tends to vary between waters but they're generally olive-green fading into a pale orange underneath, in clear weedy waters they can be bright green, in a muddy lake they can be brown. The Tench's rotund muscular body has a liberal coating of mucous (although not as much as Bream) and large powerful fins. The eye is a striking red. As a youngster I netted one for my Dad and on seeing how bright its eyes were, I asked him if the fish had batteries inside.

Emma began Tench fishing with her Dad on the 16th and has made it an annual ritual ever since. Estate lakes are the traditional homes of these fish (although you'll find bigger fish in gravel pits) and the one she's at today is on a day ticket.

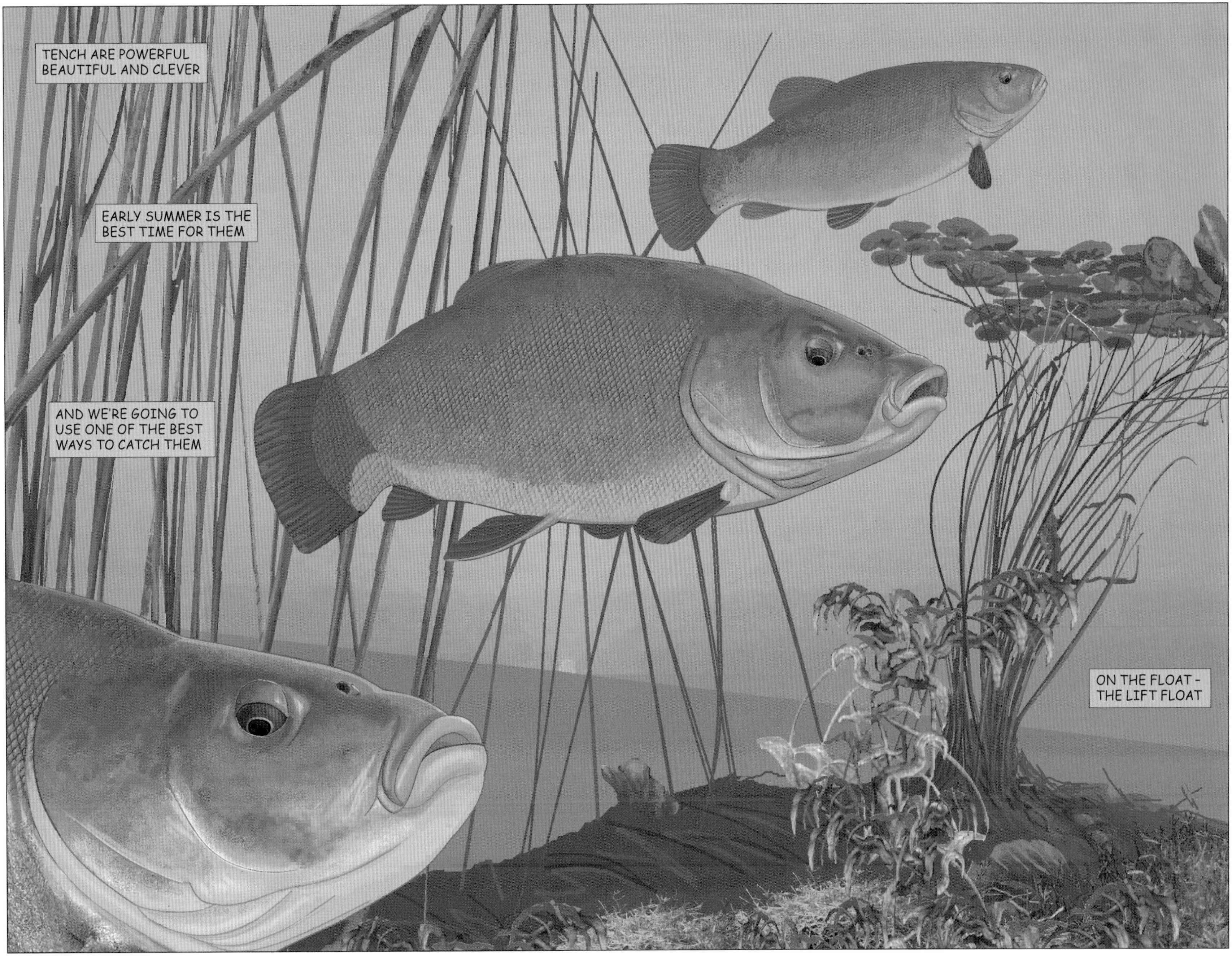
TENCH ARE POWERFUL BEAUTIFUL AND CLEVER
EARLY SUMMER IS THE BEST TIME FOR THEM
AND WE'RE GOING TO USE ONE OF THE BEST WAYS TO CATCH THEM
ON THE FLOAT - THE LIFT FLOAT

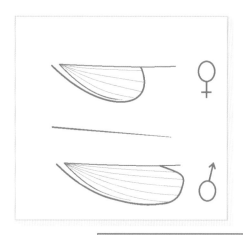

Most Coarse species can't be reliably sexed outside the breeding season but the Tench is an exception. The Pelvic fins (the paired fins between the Pectoral and Anal fins) are completely different.

The male fish has much longer, more scallop-shaped fins than the female and a pronounced ridge of muscle just above and parallel to them. This increased fin area allows a male fish to fight harder than a female. The other key difference between male and female is size: female Tench get much larger than males. Most anglers who specialise in hunting Tench reckon that the females can be double the weight of the male, so catching a 4lb male from a pond can mean that there's an 8lb female in there.

Tench are another species that have profited from the boom in Carp fishing. When I started catching them, a 6lb fish was a monster. Today this wouldn't raise many eyebrows and with a little research and organisation, a double figure fish is a real possibility.

Tench lie dormant through the winter and as the water warms in spring and the fish start to feed, they'll take quite a large bait. Traditionally Lobworm and breadflake would score, but

WITH THIS METHOD THE FLOAT IS FIXED BOTTOM END ONLY - A SINGLE SHOT ON THE BOTTOM COCKS THE FLOAT - WHEN A FISH PICKS UP THE BAIT IT LIFTS THE SHOT WHICH RELEASES THE FLOAT. A BITE IS USUALLY SIGNALLED BY THE FLOAT FALLING FLAT ONTO THE SURFACE. FOR THIS METHOD TO WORK YOU MUST ENSURE THAT YOU SET THE DEPTH CORRECTLY.

AFTER A FEW MINUTES -

THAT'S A BITE!

YEP WE'RE IN

THERE HE IS

YOU CAN SEE IT'S A MALE BY THE PELVIC FINS

nowadays small Boilies or pellets are commonly used with scaled-down Carp tactics. Later on in the season Tench become more finicky and are usually preoccupied with smaller food items which can make bait selection and presentation a lot more critical.

Emma's method today relies on a single weight to hold the float in position. When a fish picks up the bait (and moves the weight) the float is no longer held and falls flat. This is a very accurate way of fishing because if the float moves, it means the fish has the bait in its mouth. It's crucial to get the depth right so Emma plumbs up first. She uses Caster as bait and feeds lightly with Groundbait to which she's also added Casters and Hemp.

A Tench obliges soon enough but it's followed by a Bream, another Bream and finally a Rudd. It's clear that the Tench have moved on and

the bright sunlight is part of the problem. Although Tench are a fish of the summer, they are not fond of bright light so usually late mornings or early evenings are the best time to hunt them (for some reason this doesn't seem to apply to Gravel Pit Tench which can often be caught all through the day).

The 16th this year is boiling hot and although Emma got there early, the Tench soon moved to the far side of the lake and started feeding in the shadow and shade of an adjoining stone wall. She wanders over to them and drops some Groundbait and samples over the wall to the area that the fish seem to be heading towards. There's no room for her to fish though so she'll need to be able to cast to them from her current spot and to be able to do that, she'll need to change her rig.

RIGHT, I'VE HAD SOME BREAM AND THIS SWEETIE BUT THE TENCH HAVE VANISHED

SUN'S UP NOW AND IT'S BRIGHT

AND I THINK I KNOW WHERE THEY'VE GONE

THERE'S A SHOAL OF SOMETHING KICKING UP CLOUDS OF MUD AGAINST THAT SHADED WALL

I'VE BEEN TO CHECK AND THEY ARE TENCH. THERE'S NO ROOM TO SET UP OVER THERE SO WE'LL CHANGE METHOD

I'VE DROPPED SOME FREEBIES OVER THE WALL NEAR THOSE REEDS AS THE SHOAL IS MOVING IN THAT DIRECTION

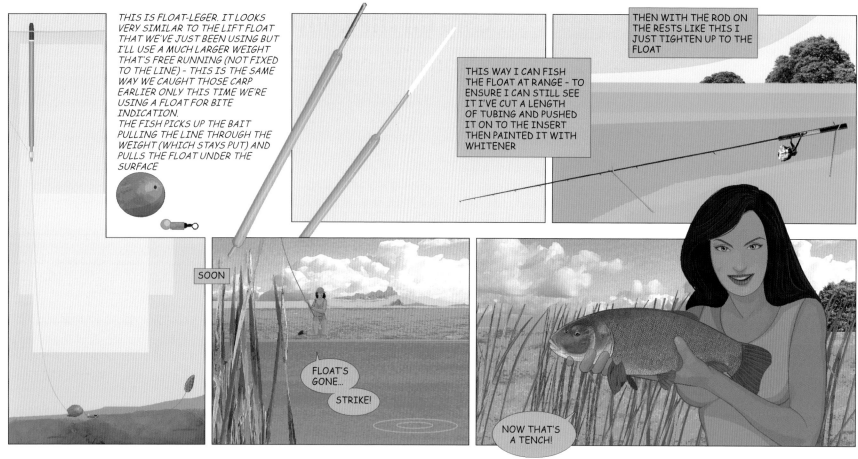

Float-leger unsurprisingly combines Float and Leger. The larger weight will allow her to cast the distance to the wall and the float will show her what's going on beneath the surface.

This method requires an accurate knowledge of the depth you're fishing but it is very versatile. It's effective here where distance is an issue and it comes into its own when high winds make normal float fishing difficult. In these conditions, the rod supported by two rests can be fished with the tip under the surface keeping the line between rod and float out of the wind.

Emma increases the size of her float by simply cutting a short length of tubing and pushing it on to the top. She paints it with Whitener (always have some in your box) so she can see it against the dark water.

It has to be said that casters aren't the easiest things to put on the hook as they burst so easily - with practice though you'll get it.
If the fish are shy try hooking them like this

We haven't talked about plastic baits yet. These can be excellent – especially those that float, as their buoyancy offsets the weight of the hook.

They're most effective when the real item is in the feed.
A plastic Caster surrounded by the real thing works a treat for Tench and is easier to put on the hook.

5. Carp on the Controller Float
Catching carp on the surface

Fishing for Carp on the surface is something that every angler must try. Watching a bobbin is one thing but to see a feeding fish taking from the surface, drifting closer and closer to your bait, then to watch its lips wrap around your bait as it's sipped from the surface, is heart-stopping. It's also a method that needs very little gear. Emma's fishing with absolute basics – but that's all she needs. This has the advantage of keeping her mobile: she can go looking for the fish rather than waiting for them to come to her. A warm south-westerly wind will often be followed by Carp looking for food. The wind is blowing into a bay at the end of the pond and it's here that Emma has set up.

She's using one of the Power float rods that she used previously and in this context it's closer to its intended purpose.

The Pellet Waggler method involves fishing a pellet under a (you've guessed it!) Waggler float. Most modern fisheries stock artificially-reared Carp which were raised on pellets. The float splashes down and the surface is regularly showered with pellets fired in small amounts from a catapult. To Carp, this is like a dinner gong: they home in on the pellets raining down around the float and sooner or later the bait gets taken as the fish compete for the food. And it's competition that is the key.

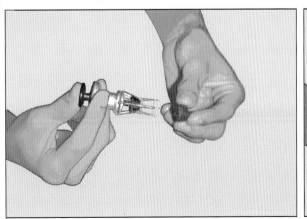

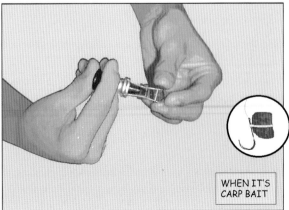

WHEN IT'S
CARP BAIT

25

Emma's using the same principle behind Pellet Waggler fishing in order to succeed with fishing from the surface.

She picks her spot, sits down quietly and starts to catapult small but regular quantities of mixer biscuits onto the surface.

The key to getting the fish to compete is getting the right amount of free food into (or onto) the swim.

As with Pellet Waggler fishing, little and often is the way to get the best results.

She doesn't fish at all, just sits quietly, patiently flicking the dog biscuits onto the surface. Then fish start to appear. Initially they just nose the bait or quietly suck it in only to quickly spit it out but then as their confidence builds, one or two of them start to feed. More biscuits drop in and more Carp come along. Seeing other Carp feeding without problem, they start to feed too. Then more fish come and as only a few of these biscuits are dropping in every minute or so, the fish start to compete for them. Bigger fish push past smaller fish, to steal the free offerings from the surface and Emma knows that it's time to start fishing.

You'll notice the Mirror Carp on the following pages look different to the one Emma encountered earlier in the year.

The lovely thing about Mirror Carp is that each fish is unique: no two scale patterns are the same. In the illustration on the following page the lower fish is a fully scaled Mirror, probably the rarest type of Mirror Carp and the fish above it has no scales at all. This is called a Leather Carp.

Leather Carp have no scales at all and are seen less frequently than other varieties. They have a much lower red blood count than other types, which can give their colouration a blue tinge and a slower growth rate, often resulting in a smaller final size than other King Carp types (although there are exceptions).

There's a lot of disagreement about what constitutes a true Leather: some say no scales at all, others that it's a Leather if the top row of scales (dorsal row) is missing or incomplete.

True Leathers are also said to have fewer rays in the Anal fin.

Emma casts her float well past the feeding fish and then gently winds it and her bait into the middle of them.

The result is instant – a hefty Mirror shoulders past two smaller fish and grabs the bait whilst it's still moving.

Realising it's hooked, the powerful fish screams off towards the middle of the lake then suddenly the line goes slack. This sometimes happens with Carp and it's natural to think that the fish is off but it can also mean that the fish has changed direction and is running towards you.

Emma knows this and because of Fishery rules she is using fairly small barbless hooks (size 12) so she has to keep the line tight or the fish will have a good chance of shedding the hook.

Fortunately she's able to do this and can then get it into open water where she can play it out.

27

The rod she is using is quite 'soft' which makes it quite forgiving as its flexibility absorbs the runs and lunges of this powerful fish.

Like many anglers targeting Carp with barbless hooks at relatively short range, Emma has learned that often only a rod with a fairly soft action has enough cushion to prevent the hook from pulling out of the fish as it surges away.

Emma gets her Carp under control, guides him to the net and he's a splendid reward for her patience.

If she stays until evening she might try another tactic that can be effective in these circumstances.

Dog mixer biscuits eventually sink and the Carp may not have got all of them. The wind has been driving the water into this bay for several hours and any uneaten biscuits will be on the marginal shelf at the far end of the bay.

Many of the older and wiser Carp have learned that the sudden and unexpected arrival of floating dog mixer biscuits in large quantities comes with a catch. Many of these fish look around for biscuits that have drifted out of the danger zone and sunk.

Often patrolling the margins in the evening they can be caught out by fishing a pre-soaked biscuit on the bottom.

As well as King Carp there are other members of the family swimming in British waters.

Wild Carp and Koi Carp are the same fish as a King Carp (they have the same Latin name) but are a different strain.

The Wild Carp looks like a long lean Common: they are fast and fight hard but don't get anywhere near as large as the other varieties and are becoming very scarce these days.

Koi Carp are an ornamental variety originating in Japan but nowadays imported from countries all over the world. They too are long and lean and exceptionally hard fighters. I've twice had the good fortune to encounter double figure Koi on light tackle – they are unforgettable.

The fish on the left is a Grass Carp, another ornamental import but a completely different species. These fish will very often come to the net without a struggle but then go ballistic when netted or on the bank – be warned!

THE STRENGTH AND POWER OF THESE FISH IS JUST AMAZING – THIS IS WHY CARP ARE SO POPULAR

THEY'VE GOT SUCH TREMENDOUS HEART

THEY NEVER GIVE UP WITHOUT A FIGHT!

OK FINALLY – THIS FISH HAS RUN ME ALL OVER THE LAKE BUT NOW...

HE'S READY

COME TO MOMMA

THAT'S FIFTEEN POUNDS OF MIRROR CARP FOR A HANDFUL OF DOG BISCUITS

6. In search of Canal Bream Silver and Bronze

Bream are deep-bodied slime-covered members of the Carp family. They favour ponds, lakes, canals and the slow flowing stretches of rivers. Emma's been pre-baiting and soon recognises the signs of a shoal of these fish. Will's struggling with a Feeder that's 'got itself tangled'. The Feeder is an excellent method for Bream at a distance but hardly necessary in a canal where bait samples and balls of Groundbait can easily be thrown in.

Bream are a shoaling fish and highly nomadic, constantly on the move looking for food so when a shoal's present they soon give themselves away. Emma knows Will needs quickly to get a bait amongst them before they move on so she shows him a method called 'Laying-on'. There are different ways of doing this but Emma goes for the most simple. Will takes a Waggler and attaches it bottom end only. The float is set overdepth and one large shot is fixed around 12 inches from the hook. The float is cocked by tightening the line when the rod is on its rests.

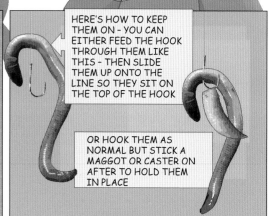

NOW DROP YOUR BAIT IN THERE

AND WE WAIT

THERE'S A LOT OF ACTIVITY OVER YOUR GROUNDBAIT

HOPEFULLY IT'LL BE BREAM –

AND YOUR BAIT IS IN THE MIDDLE OF THEM

FOR BREAM ARE VERY MUCH A SHOALING FISH

The twelve inches of line along the canal bed will allow the fish to pick up the bait without feeling any resistance.

Worms are superb for Bream but many struggle to keep this lively wriggling bait on a small barbless hook. One way is to push the hook through the worm and slide it up onto the line, then simply lower the worm back down onto the top of the hook.

Another way is to use a second bait on the hook after the worm, to hold it in place. Maggots and Casters (real or plastic) are ideal and offer a cocktail bait which is deadly for Bream.

Bream aren't the strongest or hardest of fighters but a good-sized Bream on light tackle will certainly make its presence felt.

The old advice of keeping the rod tip high when playing a fish is not helpful when barbless hooks are being used. A high rod can exert too much pressure on the hook which can pull out. So keep the rod low and exert firm and steady pressure in the form of side strain. The rod is usually only raised as the fish is drawn over the landing net.

The trick then, having caught one, is to keep the shoal around long enough to catch a few more. Fortunately Bream respond well to Ground-bait and providing the angler is careful and does nothing to spook the shoal, a good catch of fish is a real possibility. Match anglers love Bream for this reason.

For the Specimen hunter, the Bream makes a tricky but rewarding quarry. A huge humped-back Bream is an impressive sight on the bank.

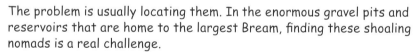

The problem is usually locating them. In the enormous gravel pits and reservoirs that are home to the largest Bream, finding these shoaling nomads is a real challenge.

Heavy pre-baiting and night fishing are both methods that often produce the best results.

The Bream in this canal are Bronze Bream or Common Bream (*Abramis brama*). A second species, the Silver Bream or White Bream (*Blicca bjoerkna*) is found in some parts of the UK, although it is much rarer and a lot smaller.

To make things even more confusing juvenile Bronze Bream are silver in colour, only turning bronze with age.

The illustration (*on the left*) shows the head of a Silver Bream. Notice how large the eye is in relation to the size of the head; the pink tinge to the Pectoral fins is also evident in the Pelvic and Anal fins and is a feature of this species.

As colours are variable, the safest way to tell a true Silver from a young Bronze is to count the number of scales along the lateral line. 44–48 and it's a Silver, 51–60 and you've got a Bronze.

7. Emma goes for gold
Rudd off the surface

Rudd are one fish that exist very much in the shadow of another. Rudd not only look like Roach but they will hybridise with them (and Bream for that matter). Where the two fish occur together, it's usually the more aggressive Roach that prospers. In Ireland for example the Rudd was king until non-native Roach were introduced and gradually the Rudd population diminished.

This is a real shame. True, small Rudd do look like small Roach but a big Rudd is one of the most stunning of Coarse fish. The silver of the young fish is replaced by a rich buttery gold, combined with wine-red fins. They fight hard too and are excellent opponents on light balanced tackle.

Emma's fishing a gravel pit, over twenty acres of rich clear water which offer these fish a perfect environment but make locating them the first job. Fortunately on a sunny day Rudd are often near the surface and these, like the Roach and Bream that we met earlier, are very much shoaling fish. Emma takes her time until she locates a shoal of good-sized fish and then, taking care not to disturb them, starts to introduce maggots with a catapult.

We've seen this before of course. Dog biscuits fired at a group of Carp caused the fish to forget their natural caution as they competed for the food. Emma wants the same result with these wary Rudd but these are wild fish and their size means that they're not youngsters. These two to three dozen fish are wise, experienced fish, survivors of a shoal of thousands and they'll be no push-over.

Emma has a small weighted Waggler which she locks with two small shot either side of the base. This will allow the bait to sink slowly and naturally (some anglers add a tiny shot just above the hooklink join). Rudd have excellent eyesight so it calls for fine line (0.08mm) and small hooks (18) again.

Rather than firing the maggots directly into the shoal, Emma's wants to get the fish moving. She fires maggots, little and often, first to their left then their right, then behind, then in front. Soon the fish are dashing backwards and forwards across the bay. Her logic is that if the fish are rushing around for the food rather than just sipping quietly from the surface, a hooked fish bolting is less likely to spook its shoal mates.

Her bait is maggots and like many anglers she likes a red and a white together on the hook for Rudd.

She fishes shallow, less than a foot of line under the clear crystal float. If the fish don't hit the bait on the drop, then she'll fire a pouch full of maggots directly at the float. As they sink around it, the arriving fish will find the freebies and the bait at a similar depth.

A variation on this technique is to fish floating maggots (or Casters). Maggots can be made to float by covering the bottom of a bait tub with water (just enough to cover the base) and dropping the maggots in. The maggots absorb air which causes them to float.

The trick once you have started catching, is not to spook the shoal. Some anglers rest the shoal after every four or five fish. They'll keep the feed going in but leave the rod out for ten minutes or so in order to allow the fish to regain their confidence.

AND THERE'S SOME REAL LUMPS AMONG THEM

NOW THE FIRST THING I NEED TO DO IS TO GET THEM ONTO MAGGOTS. THEY'RE SIPPING FLIES FROM THE SURFACE AT THE MOMENT

I'VE GOT A TUB OF MAGGOTS AND A CATAPULT - AS THE GRUBS SPLASH DOWN ONTO THE SURFACE, THE FISH WILL TURN ON THEM

THE TECHNIQUE IS THE SAME AS WHEN WE TOOK CARP OFF THE SURFACE - JUST DIFFERENT BAIT AND FINER TACKLE

I JUST KEEP A TRICKLE GOING TO GAIN THEIR CONFIDENCE AND KEEP THEM COMPETING

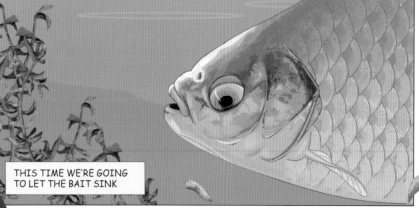

THIS TIME WE'RE GOING TO LET THE BAIT SINK

TACKLE COULDN'T BE SIMPLER: A WEIGHTED WAGGLER AND A HOOK

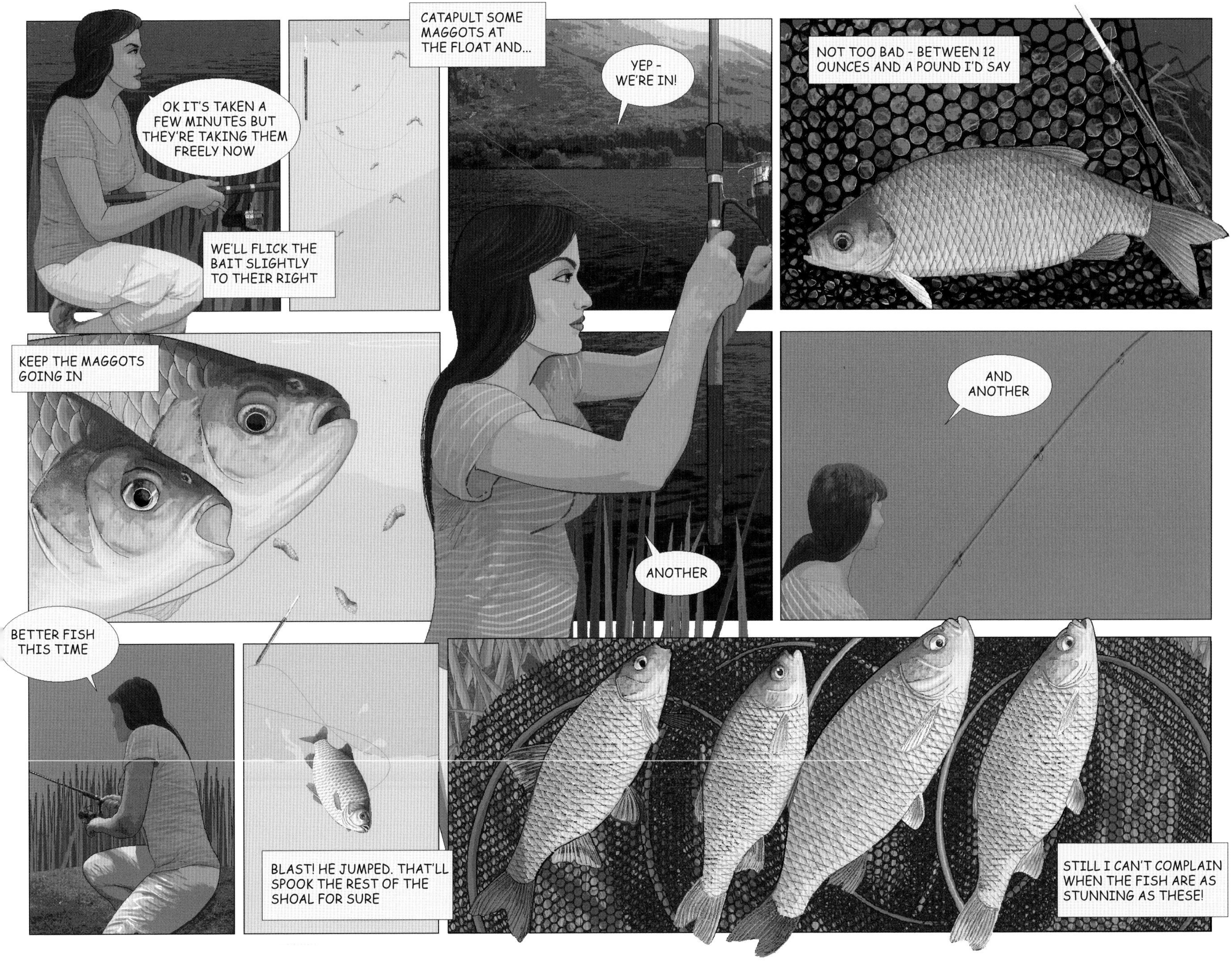
OK IT'S TAKEN A FEW MINUTES BUT THEY'RE TAKING THEM FREELY NOW
WE'LL FLICK THE BAIT SLIGHTLY TO THEIR RIGHT
CATAPULT SOME MAGGOTS AT THE FLOAT AND...
YEP - WE'RE IN!
NOT TOO BAD - BETWEEN 12 OUNCES AND A POUND I'D SAY
KEEP THE MAGGOTS GOING IN
ANOTHER
AND ANOTHER
BETTER FISH THIS TIME
BLAST! HE JUMPED. THAT'LL SPOOK THE REST OF THE SHOAL FOR SURE
STILL I CAN'T COMPLAIN WHEN THE FISH ARE AS STUNNING AS THESE!

8. A difficult fish from a hard place
Emma goes in search of Crucians

The Crucian Carp resembles a short plump Common Carp without the barbels. These hardy little Carp arrived in the UK long before the King Carp and despite their ability to survive low temperatures they are truly a fish of the summer.

They're also awkward. These are some of the most shy biting fish that the Coarse angler will encounter and they love cover, so are rarely found far from snags. Any angler taking on one of these little characters needs to think carefully about their set-up. Emma's method borrows heavily from

The hook is threaded through the eye and pushed into the cork of the Plummet. The float can be slid up or down the line.
Left: Float too close to hook – too shallow
Middle: Float too far from hook – too deep
Right: Depth correct

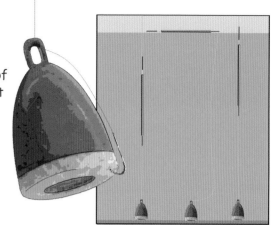

CRUCIAN CARP LOVE COVER

I'M TRYING FOR A CRUCIAN THIS MORNING AND THE LILIES CLOSE TO THE BANK LOOK PROMISING

SO WE NEED TO WORK OUT HOW TO EXTRACT ONE FROM SUCH A TRICKY SPOT

BAIT IS A SMALL RED WORM

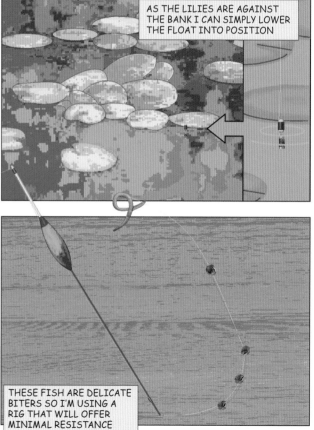

AS THE LILIES ARE AGAINST THE BANK I CAN SIMPLY LOWER THE FLOAT INTO POSITION

THESE FISH ARE DELICATE BITERS SO I'M USING A RIG THAT WILL OFFER MINIMAL RESISTANCE

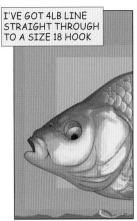

I'VE GOT 4LB LINE STRAIGHT THROUGH TO A SIZE 18 HOOK

THE KEY HERE IS TO GET THE DEPTH RIGHT - THE BOTTOM SHOT COCKS THE FLOAT AND MUST BE ON THE BOTTOM

AS SOON AS THE FISH PICKS UP THE BAIT THE SHOT IS LIFTED OFF THE BOTTOM...

AND WE'RE IN!

THE TIGHT CLUTCH KEEPS THE FISH OUT OF THE LILIES

THE SOFT ROD CUSHIONS THE HOOK

I JUST NEED TO KEEP HIM IN THE OPEN WATER AWAY FROM THE LILIES

SOON

RIGHT, HE'S READY FOR THE LANDING NET

AND THERE HE IS!

Pole fishing and has rapidly become popular with Crucian hunters: a long flexible rod, reel with the clutch set fairly tight and a pole float set up as shown. It's extremely sensitive. For this to work, the lowest shot must be on the pool bottom so finding the correct depth is vital. Fortunately fishing so close to the bank with a long rod makes plumbing the depth simply a matter of lowering the plummet into the water under the rod tip and it won't disturb the swim. This delicate Pole float needs four small shot to cock it. The bottom shot is close to the bait, so as the fish picks it up, the shot is dislodged and the float moves. Emma strikes at the slightest movement of the float as the bait will be in the fish's mouth.

An advantage in this particular pond is the absence of King Carp and Tench, who favour the same habitat and baits as the smaller Crucian.

Emma's bait is a little unconventional for Crucian Carp. The usual choice might be Caster, maggot, corn or pellet. Emma's had good results here before with small Redworms so that's what she's using today. The long rod and proximity of the lilies to the bank allow Emma to lower the bait into the exact spot she wants, right up against the lily pads.

When a fish is hooked, it bolts for the lily as Emma pulls against it. Normally a small barbless hook would be in danger of pulling out of the fish's mouth, but the softness and 'give' of the rod acts as a cushion and prevents this from happening. She's able to keep the powerful little fish bouncing around under the rod tip until it's ready for the net.

Nowadays, wild Goldfish (Brown Goldfish) are often mistaken for Crucian Carp. They are difficult to tell apart at the best of times and the fact that both species hybridise makes things even more complicated. Lateral line scale count is generally: Goldfish 27–29 and Crucian 32–34.

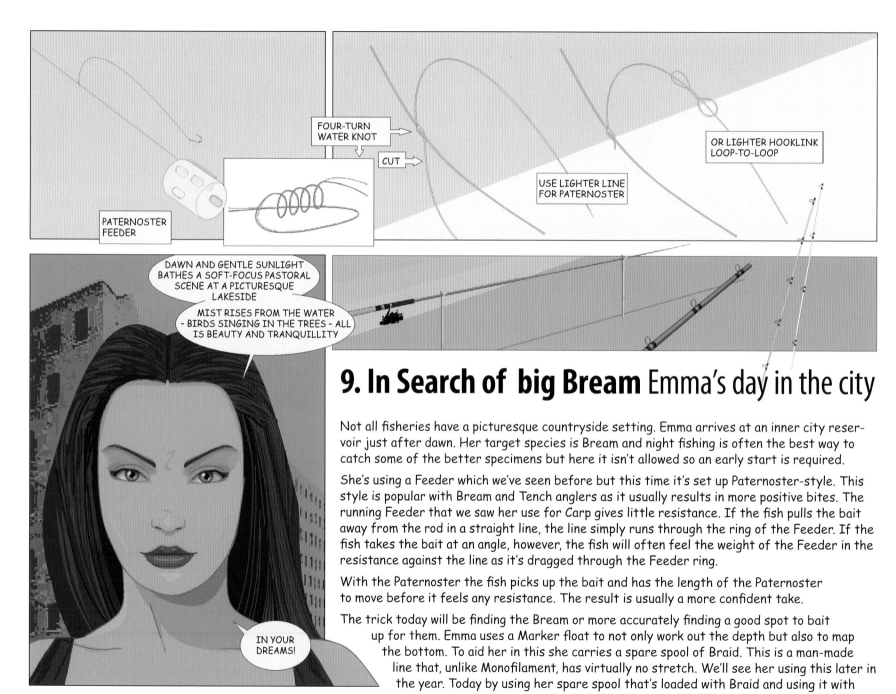

FOUR-TURN
WATER KNOT

CUT

OR LIGHTER HOOKLINK
LOOP-TO-LOOP

USE LIGHTER LINE
FOR PATERNOSTER

PATERNOSTER
FEEDER

DAWN AND GENTLE SUNLIGHT
BATHES A SOFT-FOCUS PASTORAL
SCENE AT A PICTURESQUE
LAKESIDE

MIST RISES FROM THE WATER
– BIRDS SINGING IN THE TREES – ALL
IS BEAUTY AND TRANQUILLITY

IN YOUR
DREAMS!

9. In Search of big Bream Emma's day in the city

Not all fisheries have a picturesque countryside setting. Emma arrives at an inner city reservoir just after dawn. Her target species is Bream and night fishing is often the best way to catch some of the better specimens but here it isn't allowed so an early start is required.

She's using a Feeder which we've seen before but this time it's set up Paternoster-style. This style is popular with Bream and Tench anglers as it usually results in more positive bites. The running Feeder that we saw her use for Carp gives little resistance. If the fish pulls the bait away from the rod in a straight line, the line simply runs through the ring of the Feeder. If the fish takes the bait at an angle, however, the fish will often feel the weight of the Feeder in the resistance against the line as it's dragged through the Feeder ring.

With the Paternoster the fish picks up the bait and has the length of the Paternoster to move before it feels any resistance. The result is usually a more confident take.

The trick today will be finding the Bream or more accurately finding a good spot to bait up for them. Emma uses a Marker float to not only work out the depth but also to map the bottom. To aid her in this she carries a spare spool of Braid. This is a man-made line that, unlike Monofilament, has virtually no stretch. We'll see her using this later in the year. Today by using her spare spool that's loaded with Braid and using it with

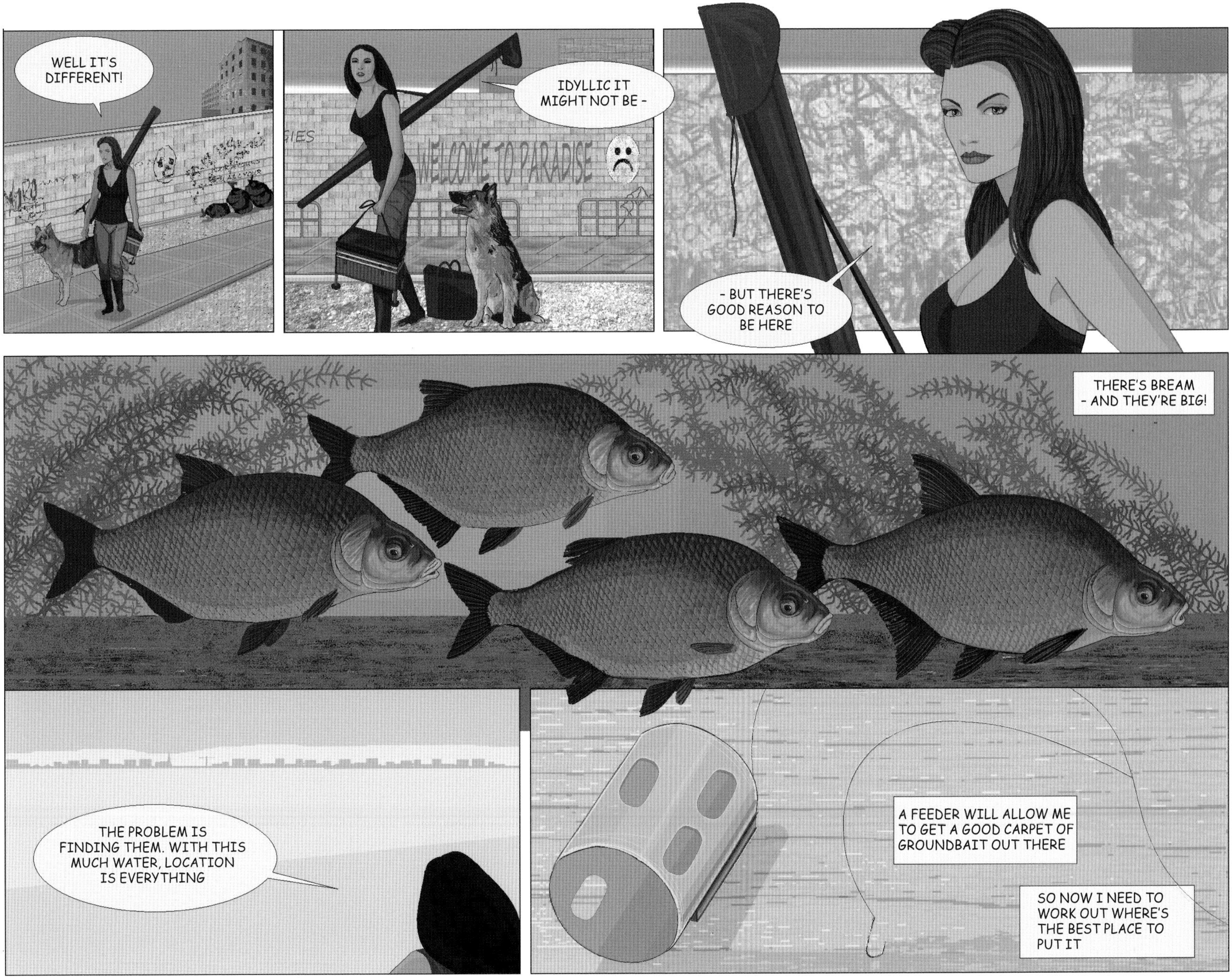
WELL IT'S DIFFERENT!
IDYLLIC IT MIGHT NOT BE -
WELCOME TO PARADISE
- BUT THERE'S GOOD REASON TO BE HERE
THERE'S BREAM - AND THEY'RE BIG!
THE PROBLEM IS FINDING THEM. WITH THIS MUCH WATER, LOCATION IS EVERYTHING
A FEEDER WILL ALLOW ME TO GET A GOOD CARPET OF GROUNDBAIT OUT THERE
SO NOW I NEED TO WORK OUT WHERE'S THE BEST PLACE TO PUT IT

THIS IS A MARKER FLOAT – I'VE RUN THE LINE UNTIED THROUGH THE LEAD AND THEN TIED THE FLOAT TO THE END OF THE LINE

I LOB IT OUT INTO THE LAKE

THEN WIND THE FLOAT BACK TO THE WEIGHT

NOW WHEN I PULL A FOOT OF LINE OFF THE REEL AT THIS END

AS YOU WIND THE RIG BACK IN YOU START TO GET AN IDEA OF WHAT'S ON THE BOTTOM

SO NOW I JUST COUNT IT UP – THREE, FOUR – THERE'S THE FLOAT ON FIVE. IT'S FIVE FEET DEEP THERE

I KNOW THAT THE MARKER FLOAT RISES UP BY A FOOT AT THE OTHER END

YOU FEEL THE WEIGHT KNOCKING AND BOUNCING ACROSS GRAVEL

FEEL IT DRAGGING THROUGH MUD AND SILT

OR FEEL IT CATCHING AND PULLING THROUGH A WEEDBED

YOU CAN SOON BUILD UP A MAP

ONCE I'VE FOUND MY SPOT

I PICK A POINT ON THE HORIZON LIKE THAT CRANE...

...AND CAST TO IT

NOW I'M WHERE I WANT TO BE, I TUCK THE LINE UNDER THE LINE CLIP

THEN NEXT CAST I'LL AIM AT THE CRANE AS I CAST AND THE CLIP WILL STOP THE LINE AT THE SAME DISTANCE

BY MAPPING THE WATER WE CAN WORK OUT THE BEST AREAS TO FISH. THE TECHNIQUE WE'RE USING RELIES ON BUILDING UP A FEEDING AREA FOR THE FISH – THIS WILL TAKE TIME AND EFFORT SO WE NEED TO ENSURE THAT WE PICK A GOOD AREA TO FEED TO BEGIN WITH.
BREAM ARE OFTEN FURTHER FROM THE SHORE THAN OTHER SPECIES AND THEY DON'T TEND TO FEED IN WEEDBEDS – THERE'S LOTS OF WEED OUT THERE AHEAD OF US BUT THERE'S ALSO GRAVEL, MUD AND SILT.
THE MARKER FLOAT LETS ME MAP THE BOTTOM AND CHOOSE THE BEST PLACE TO PUT MY BAIT.
ONCE I'VE CAST OUT MY RIG I PUT MY ROD ON THE RESTS AND TIGHTEN UP. THIS WILL PUT A SLIGHT BEND INTO THE QUIVERTIP AS THIS IS AT AN ANGLE TO THE BAIT – A BITE WILL PULL THE TIP AROUND AS THE LIGHTNESS OF THE TIP HELPS TO GREATLY MAGNIFY THE BITE.

the Marker she feels every bump and snag as she retrieves. Once she's got an idea of the ground before her, she needs only to swap the spool of Braid for a spool of Mono and she's ready to go. Emma recasts every 15 minutes or so. If she can hit the same spot every time, this builds up a bed of food to draw and hold the Bream shoal. To get this accuracy she could have put the Marker float on a spare rod and used it as a target for her fishing rod. Instead she picks a target on the horizon to give her a line and the reel clip to set the distance.

She casts towards the crane to an area she's identified with the Marker float, then she tucks the line under the line clip and winds in. Now when she casts again at the crane, the line clip will drop the bait and rig onto the same spot. But using the line clip in this way does have its disadvantages. A Bream taking the bait won't put too much of a strain on the line, but a Carp roaring off with it is a different matter.

A powerful fish wrenching the line against the clip will break the line unless great care is taken.

Emma's using a Feeder rod that comes with several Quivertips. A Quivertip is a delicate rod tip that plugs into the top of the main rod. It offers minimal resistance to a taking fish, so bites are very obvious, especially if the rod is set up at an angle to the water (rather than pointing directly at the bait).

Emma's using Groundbait in the Feeder and if there's one species that's synonymous with Groundbait then it's Bream. Right now, fishmeal Groundbaits are popular, often mixed with brown crumb, and this is the base of Emma's mix. She's also added leftovers from her last few trips: maggots, Squats, Hemp, sweetcorn and some micro pellets. Hookbait will be a cocktail based on these ingredients. Her approach then, is to

THAT SENSITIVE TIP WILL CLEARLY SHOW ME IF ANYTHING PICKS UP THE BAIT

NOW BREAM LOVE GROUND-BAIT AND I'VE GOT LOTS HERE - IT'S A FISHMEAL BASE WITH LOTS OF ADDITIONS

I PRESS IT INTO THE FEEDER - GETTING A GOOD HELPING IN

THE WATER BREAKS IT DOWN

I'LL RE-CAST EVERY FIFTEEN MINUTES OR SO FOR THE FIRST HOUR OR TWO. SHOALS OF BREAM ARE NOMADIC, CONSTANTLY ROAMING AROUND LOOKING FOR FOOD

HOPEFULLY THEY'LL FIND THE GROUNDBAIT AND IT'LL KEEP THE SHOAL ROOTING AROUND LOOKING FOR MORE

pick her spot, build up a bed of food and then ambush the Bream as they arrive. The Marker float revealed a long gravel bar beyond the weedbed. This becomes her fishing ground. She mixes her Groundbait at the reservoir preferring to use the water from the venue she's fishing. The mix needs to be firm enough to stay with the Feeder on the cast but soft enough to break down quickly as it sinks.

So it's: fill the Feeder, cast out, retrieve after 15 minutes, refill and cast back to the same spot. The first fish to arrive are Roach and a small Eel but not long after, the Bream start to arrive.

Her first is around 4lb. It would be a cracking fish from the canal but here it's only average. But it's quickly followed by another and then another and this of course is one of the main attractions of Bream

fishing: once you've got a shoal in residence then, providing you're careful, a bumper catch is a real possibility.

Several hours later Emma eventually runs out of bait (a surprisingly common problem for anglers connecting with a shoal of Bream). The reservoir is a bit of a trek from the nearest parking and this limits the amount of tackle and bait she can bring with her.

Not that this will worry her. Today's adventure has ended with a new P.B. for Emma. A big Bream on the bank is a truly spectacular thing, and this double-figure Bream is just such a fish and is a rewarding end to a demanding day.

HERE WE GO

WELL IT'S BEEN AN HOUR – I'VE HAD A FEW ROACH AND A TINY EEL BUT THIS FEELS LIKE A BREAM

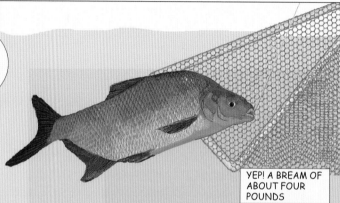

YEP! A BREAM OF ABOUT FOUR POUNDS

AND ANOTHER

THIS ONE'S A LITTLE SMALLER

A FEW HOURS LATER

WELL I'VE HAD A CRACKING DAY – DOZENS OF BREAM TO ABOUT SIX POUNDS - WITH ONE EXCEPTION...

HAVE A LOOK AT THIS – TEN POUND THREE! IT'S MY FIRST DOUBLE-FIGURE BREAM

LOOK AT THIS FISH!

ARE YOU SITTING COMFORTABLY? GOOD - BECAUSE THINGS ARE ABOUT TO GET COMPLICATED

MANY MATCH ANGLERS USE THE PELLET WAGGLER TO CATCH SPECTACULAR WEIGHTS OF SUMMER CARP. IT'S A TECHNIQUE THAT REQUIRES A LOT OF WORK FROM THE ANGLER, REGULARLY CATAPULTING PELLETS TO THE FLOAT WHERE THE PELLET BAIT IS FISHED HIGH IN THE WATER. THE MORE OFTEN YOU FEED, THE HIGHER THE FISH WILL RISE. COMPETING CARP WILL BE ATTRACTED TO THE SOUND OF PELLETS HITTING THE SURFACE AND WILL BATTLE TO GET AT THE FREEBIES SLOWLY SINKING AROUND THE HOOKBAIT.
ONE OF THESE CARP WILL SOONER OR LATER GRAB THE BAIT. THE TRICK IS TO LEARN TO FIRE THE CATAPULT WHILST KEEPING HOLD OF THE ROD AND TO CHOOSE PELLETS THAT DON'T SINK TOO QUICKLY (LOW OIL ARE BEST).
THE FEEDER FLOAT ON THE RIGHT IS A BAGGING WAGGLER. GROUNDBAIT IS PRESSED ONTO THE FRAME BELOW THE FLOAT WHICH, ON HITTING THE WATER, BREAKS DOWN LEAVING A FALLING TRAIL AROUND THE HOOKBAIT.

10. Emma rigs up to catch Carp

Back in the second chapter we looked at simple running rigs for Carp. Today it's Fixed rigs or Bolt rigs. Modern Carp fishing is both science and art and to the newcomer can appear extremely complicated.

To cover everything we'd need an entire book so we're aiming just to give you an overview. The earlier set-ups we used catch Carp and are perfect for short sessions but for longer sessions or night sessions, sitting for hours on end staring at a pair of bobbins just isn't practical. We've already told you how Bolt rigs work. The crucial thing is to ensure a Bolt rig is safe. If your main line breaks for any reason, a safe rig will allow the fish to free itself of the lead weight. Otherwise the fish will drag the weight around with it until it gets tangled up and dies, tethered to a snag. Safe rigs are usually achieved with a semi-fixed lead, where the weight is fixed in a clip but will pull out easily if the weight jams.

METHOD FEEDERS VARY IN SHAPE AND SIZE BUT ALL PROVIDE A FRAME FOR A STIFF GROUNDBAIT MIX (A SPECIFIC 'METHOD MIX' ONE). THE USUAL WAY IS TO PRESS SOME GROUNDBAIT HARD ONTO THE FEEDER FRAME UNTIL IT'S COVERED. THE BAIT IS PRESSED INTO THIS AND THEN A TOP COATING OF GROUNDBAIT IS PRESSED LIGHTLY (BUT FIRM ENOUGH TO SURVIVE THE CAST) OVER THE LAYER OF BAIT. THIS MAKES A BALL WITH THE BAIT AT THE CENTRE. ON HITTING THE WATER THE FEEDER SINKS AND THE OUTER (LIGHTLY COMPRESSED) LAYER OF GROUNDBAIT BREAKS DOWN LEAVING THE BAIT SITTING ON A MOUND OF GROUNDBAIT.
THIS TECHNIQUE IS SO POPULAR THAT MANY (ESPECIALLY LARGER) CARP HAVE STARTED TO WISE UP TO IT. THE BAIT IS, AFTER ALL, VERY CLOSE TO THE FEEDER AND CARP AREN'T STUPID. ON HARD-FISHED COMMERCIALS THE METHOD WILL USUALLY CATCH THE MOST CARP BUT NOT THE BIGGEST ONES.
ONE WAY AROUND THIS IS TO USE TEXTURED OR NATURAL LEADS, RESEMBLING STONES. THESE TEND TO AROUSE LESS SUSPICION AND WILL TAKE A STIFF MIX.

THE RIG HOOKS THE FISH WHICH INSTANTLY BOLTS – A 'BAITRUNNER' TYPE REEL ALLOWS THE FISH TO TAKE LINE AS AN AUDIBLE ALARM SIGNALS A RUN. THE ANGLER DOESN'T NEED TO STRIKE (AS THE FISH IS ALREADY HOOKED) – THEY SIMPLY PICK UP THE ROD, TURNING THE REEL HANDLE WHICH ENGAGES THE REEL'S CLUTCH AND THE FISH CAN BE PLAYED AS NORMAL.

MODERN CARP FISHERS OFTEN USE MULTIPLE ROD SET-UPS

STATE-OF-THE-ART RIGS

WEEKEND, WEEK-LONG OR EVEN LONGER SESSIONS

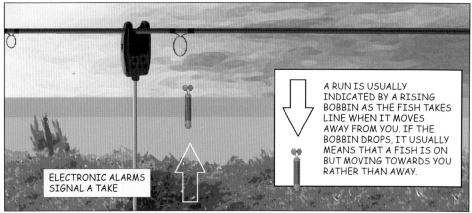

CARP IN THE UK ARE BIGGER NOW THAN THEY HAVE EVER BEEN

AND CARP GEAR IS MORE SOPHISTICATED THAN EVER

ELECTRONIC ALARMS SIGNAL A TAKE

A RUN IS USUALLY INDICATED BY A RISING BOBBIN AS THE FISH TAKES LINE WHEN IT MOVES AWAY FROM YOU. IF THE BOBBIN DROPS, IT USUALLY MEANS THAT A FISH IS ON BUT MOVING TOWARDS YOU RATHER THAN AWAY.

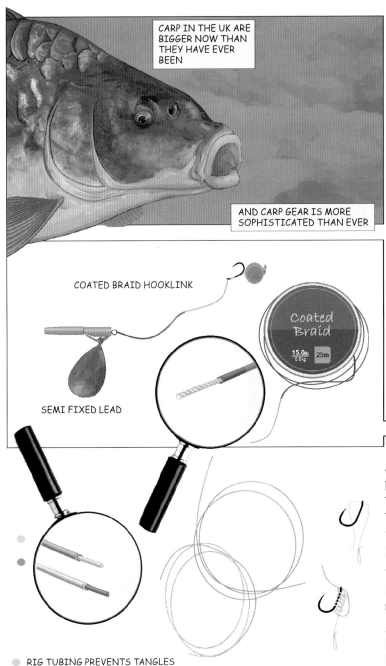

COATED BRAID HOOKLINK

SEMI FIXED LEAD

Coated Braid

15.0lb 6.8kg 25m

RIG TUBING PREVENTS TANGLES

LEADCORE SINKING LINE

A SUPPLE BRAID HOOKLINK IS COATED IN A STIFF (USUALLY PLASTIC) MATERIAL WHICH CAN BE PEELED BACK SO YOU HAVE THE SUPPLE MOBILE BRAID AT THE HOOK FOR OUTSTANDING BAIT PRESENTATION

AND THEN THICKER COATED BRAID AT THE SWIVEL WON'T TANGLE UP

Most Carp baits today are presented on a hair rig which allows the bait to sit near the hook as opposed to on it.

The easiest way to tie a Hair rig is with a knotless knot.

This technique is usually associated with Boilie or pellet baits but works well with many other baits.

A baiting needle will enable you to get the Boilie onto the hair and once in place it can be held there by a Boilie stop, a smaller bait item or even a blade of grass.

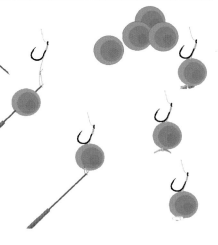

THIS IS A PVA MESH BAG - I'VE FILLED IT WITH CRUSHED PELLET AND I SLIP IT ONTO THE HOOK LIKE THIS

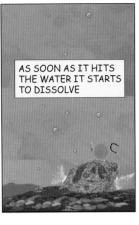

AS SOON AS IT HITS THE WATER IT STARTS TO DISSOLVE

SOON ALL THAT'S LEFT IS YOUR BAIT AND A NEAT PILE OF CRUSHED PELLET

THAT GOT ME THIS LOVELY LOW-TO-MID DOUBLE COMMON

AND THIS MIRROR A FEW OUNCES BIGGER FELL TO A PVA STRINGER

THIN STRANDS OF PVA MAKE UP A CORD - ONTO THIS A NUMBER OF FREE OFFERINGS CAN BE THREADED - IT IS THEN ATTACHED TO THE HOOK AND IN THE WATER IT SOON DISSOLVES LEAVING OFFERINGS ALONGSIDE BAIT.

PVA (Poly Vinyl Alcohol) is very much a part of modern Carp fishing.

It is available in several forms: clear bags, mesh bags, string or tape. Whichever type you use will dissolve underwater leaving its contents beside your hookbait.

Clear bags can be filled with free offerings as well as the hookbait and weight and then sealed (make a few holes in the bag to let the air out). Mesh bags use a woven PVA thread. They can be made up very quickly and easily and won't trap air.

PVA tape can be used to tie off and seal the clear bags or (as with PVA string) used to make a Stringer.

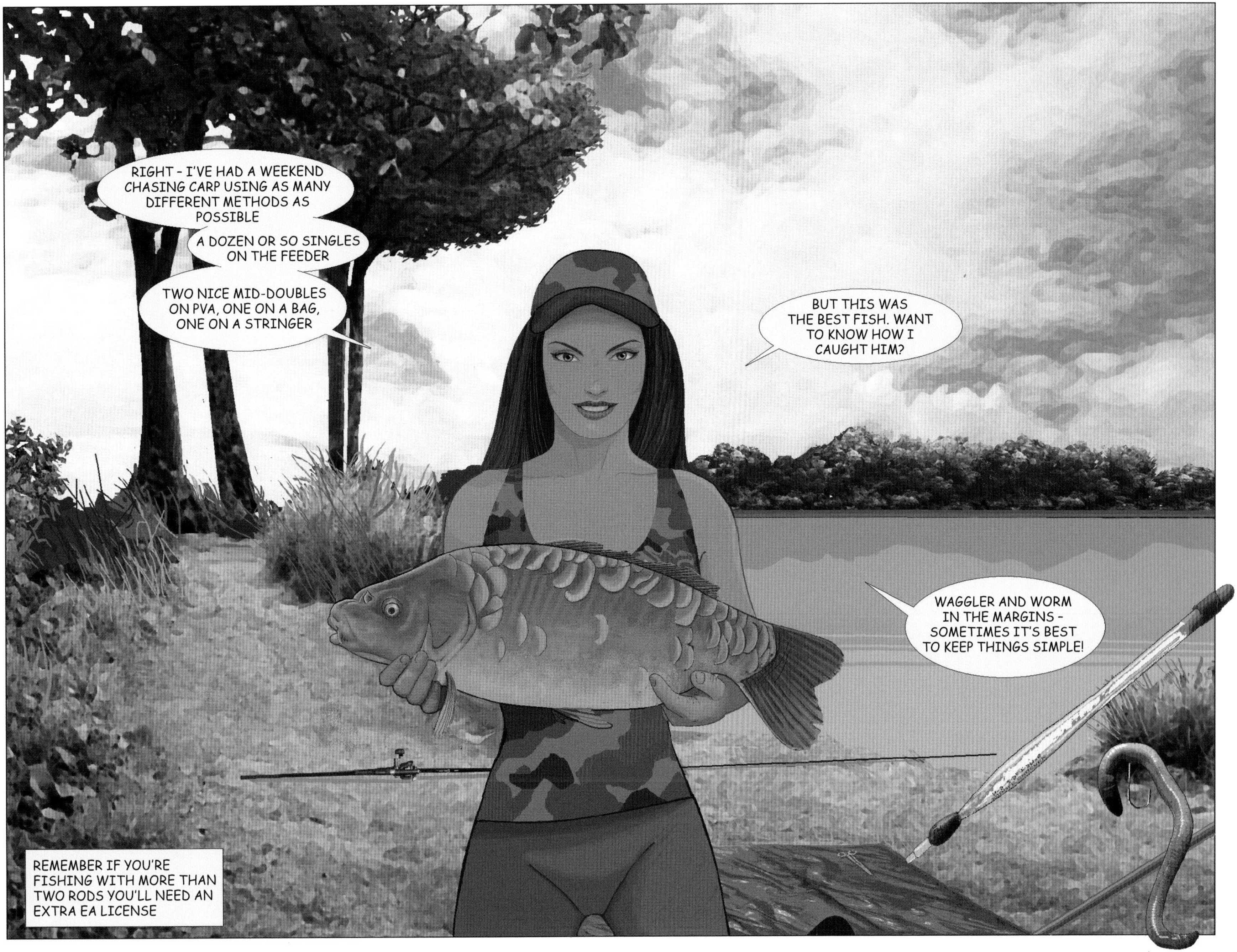
RIGHT - I'VE HAD A WEEKEND CHASING CARP USING AS MANY DIFFERENT METHODS AS POSSIBLE
A DOZEN OR SO SINGLES ON THE FEEDER
TWO NICE MID-DOUBLES ON PVA, ONE ON A BAG, ONE ON A STRINGER
BUT THIS WAS THE BEST FISH. WANT TO KNOW HOW I CAUGHT HIM?
WAGGLER AND WORM IN THE MARGINS - SOMETIMES IT'S BEST TO KEEP THINGS SIMPLE!
REMEMBER IF YOU'RE FISHING WITH MORE THAN TWO RODS YOU'LL NEED AN EXTRA EA LICENSE

11. Emma's night out (with a slippery guy)

Emma's target in this chapter is the mysterious Eel. She knows that fishing a neglected lake on a warm muggy night gives her a chance of catching one of these amazing creatures.

Night fishing though is not easy and her target species is no push-over either. Preparation is the key to success so she chooses her swim in daylight, making a mental note of snags in the water and obstacles on the bank. Then she pre-baits a shallow marginal shelf with dead maggots. Eels, pound for pound, are one of the strongest fish in freshwater and one of the hardest to handle on the bank. She chooses a strong twelve foot Carp rod teamed with a robust reel and will fish a worm bait, Touch legered over the dead maggots.

Touch legering involves fishing with the line looped around a finger. Despite the fact that she's fishing at close range, she'll strike the bite the second she feels it. Her reason is that she's looking for a big Eel. If a small Eel picks up her worm it'll take a few moments for the fish to get the bait properly in its mouth and a fast strike will most likely pull the bait (and the hook) out of its mouth. A big Eel, on the other hand, will simply 'hoover' up the worm in one motion and a fast strike will ensure that the fish is hooked in the front of the mouth before it can swallow the bait.

Eels are one of those fish (like Pike) that look very robust and strong but are in fact quite easily injured on the bank and sadly, nowadays, Eels are rare.

This never used to be the case and for many anglers of my generation (myself included) Eels were their first fish.

The experience was usually the same: the float would disappear leaving an unseen thing tugging and pulling at the line. Hands trembling with excitement you'd grab rod and reel handle, tugging and turning until the culprit was swung onto the bank. There instead of the expected flashing silver Roach or bristling striped Perch, would be a glistening snake-like creature dripping with slime and with an uncanny ability to tie itself and your tackle into a tangled bird's nest of knots. This mess would then (in my case anyway) be handed triumphantly to Dad to unhook and sort out.

Eels were everywhere you fished in those days: these were 'Yellow Eels', the freshwater form of *Anguilla anguilla*. The sea-going form is called the 'Silver'. Wherever there was water, it seemed, there were Eels.

And then the Eels were gone, the population collapsed. There are many theories and the most likely cause is a parasite *Anguillicoloides crassus* which crossed over from the Japanese Eel which had been imported for food, but some of which escaped (Eels are good at that!) and mixed with native European Eels. The parasite destroys the European Eel's swim bladder. The fish start their lives in the deep waters south of Bermuda 3000 miles away and without a swim bladder the return journey becomes impossible. The impact of the loss of the Eel has many consequences and some are only just becoming apparent. Eels are a 'keystone species': they impact disproportionately on other species around them such as cormorants and otters. Eels made up a huge part of their diet so they were forced to turn to other species with disastrous and far-reaching consequences.

From the angler's point of view, as with so many of our freshwater species, a juvenile Eel is a completely different prospect to a specimen.

49

A specimen Eel is unforgettable, a 'once in a lifetime fish'. They say that for every pound an Eel weighs, it's ten years old. Now the current record is over thirteen pounds so to hold a big Eel is to hold something that is probably older than you.

And it's when you're holding them that the fun really begins. A small Eel's a nightmare, so what on earth would a big one be like?

Well, big Eels attract a certain kind of angler. Fishing (usually at night) these anglers have put in hundreds or even thousands of hours and have turned hunting and handling these fish into an art-form. The trick is: don't fight the Eel. An old tale states if eels are laid on their backs, they would lie there until they died. And it's actually true: for some reason an Eel laid on its back won't move. Of course, it's easier said than done.

The experts lie the Eel on a damp unhooking mat and cover its eyes with a wet weighing bag or cloth. Gently stroke the sides of the Eel as this helps to calm them down. Handle the Eel gently and confidently (again easily said but it really does work) and roll it onto its back. The hook can then be removed with forceps.

Disgorgers should only be used with extreme care (many find the 'Slammer' type best for Eels). If the fish is deeply hooked it's probably better to cut the line as near to the hook as possible, as Eels have a knack of coughing them up on their own.

Disgorgers are not a good idea because most of the fish's vital organs are directly behind the head and are easily damaged unless great care is taken. Eels need to be handled with great care and if possible, fish with somebody who's got experience in handling them or visit the websites of the groups that specialise in this species. Many have video tutorials that show experts demonstrating how to handle these fish.

It is said that for every hundred Eels alive in the 1970s, there's one alive today. The Eel population has been almost wiped out. Whether or not they will be able to recover is unknown but any Eel caught should be handled and returned as quickly and carefully as possible.

Big Eels are still out there and are intelligent and powerful opponents.

Emma's Eel isn't the 5lb one that she's sought for years but it's still a super fish. Sitting quietly in the moonlight, watching, waiting, then feeling the bite and fighting this creature of darkness and mystery, finally winning the battle and holding the prize, makes this difficult and demanding style of fishing an unforgettable adventure. You are looking into the moonlit eyes of a creature born two hundred metres deep in the seas off the Bermuda Triangle. A creature that that has changed its shape as it travelled through treacherous waters for thousands of miles, that has hunted, fed and grown for forty or fifty years until the day it grabs your bait. A creature that will fight you every inch of the way to the net that lifts it from its inky black home, is one of the amazing experiences that make angling all that it is.

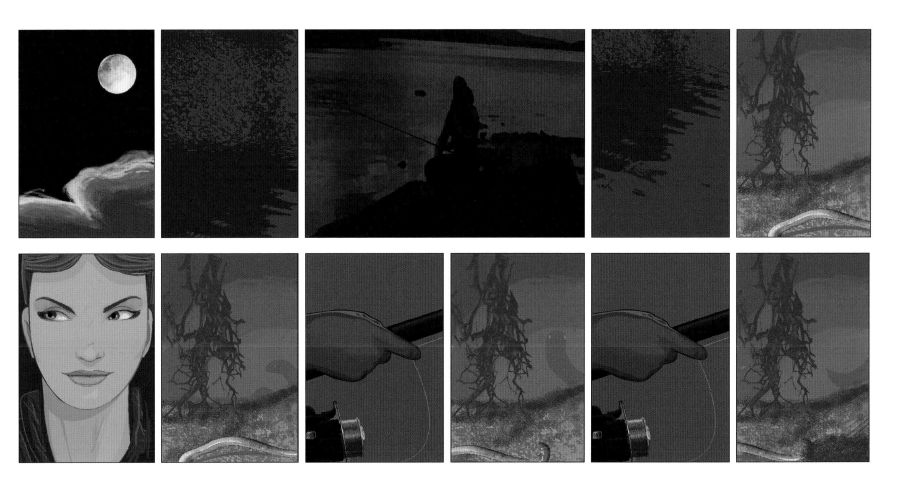

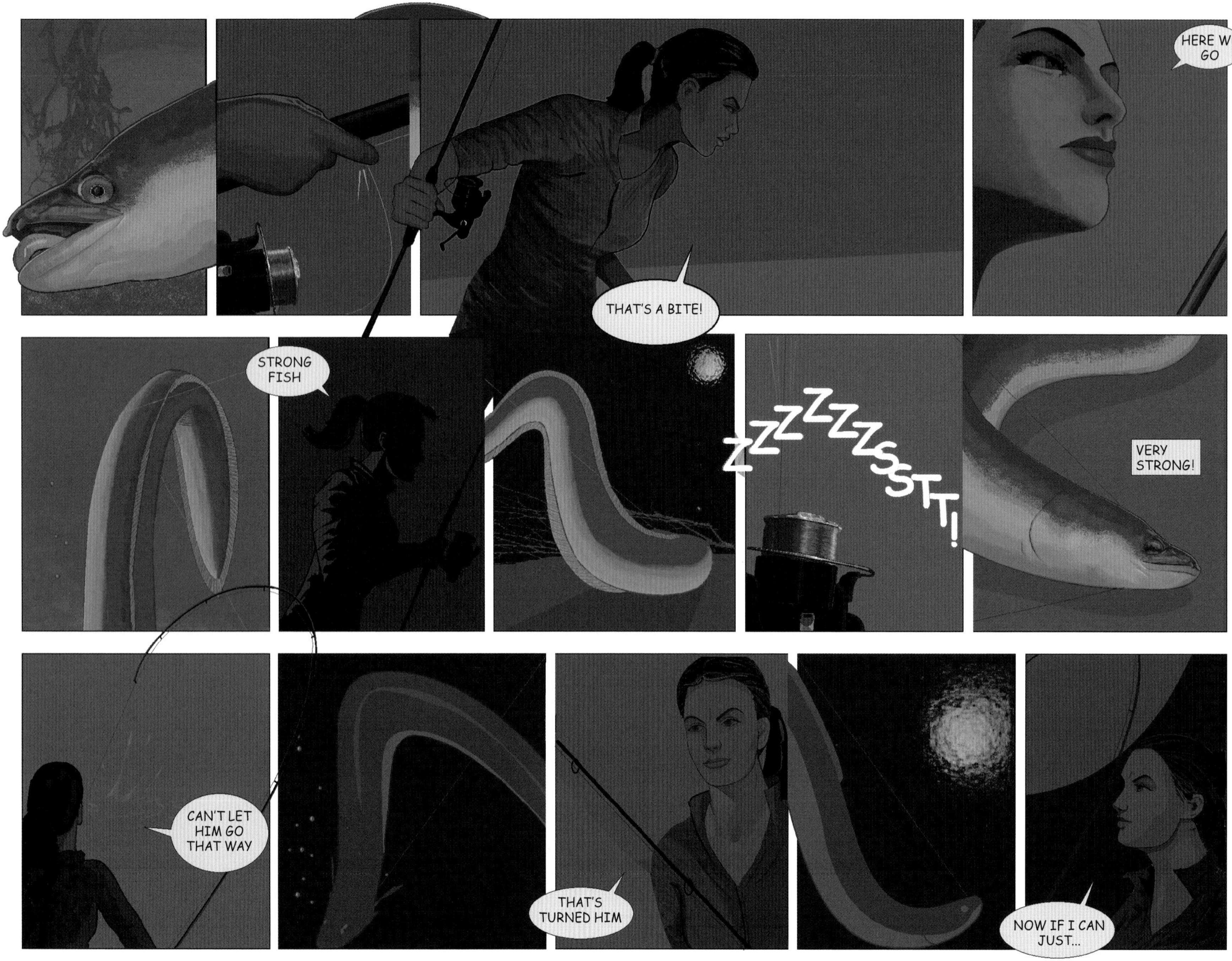
HERE WE GO
THAT'S A BITE!
STRONG FISH
ZZZZZZZSSSTTT!
VERY STRONG!
CAN'T LET HIM GO THAT WAY
THAT'S TURNED HIM
NOW IF I CAN JUST...

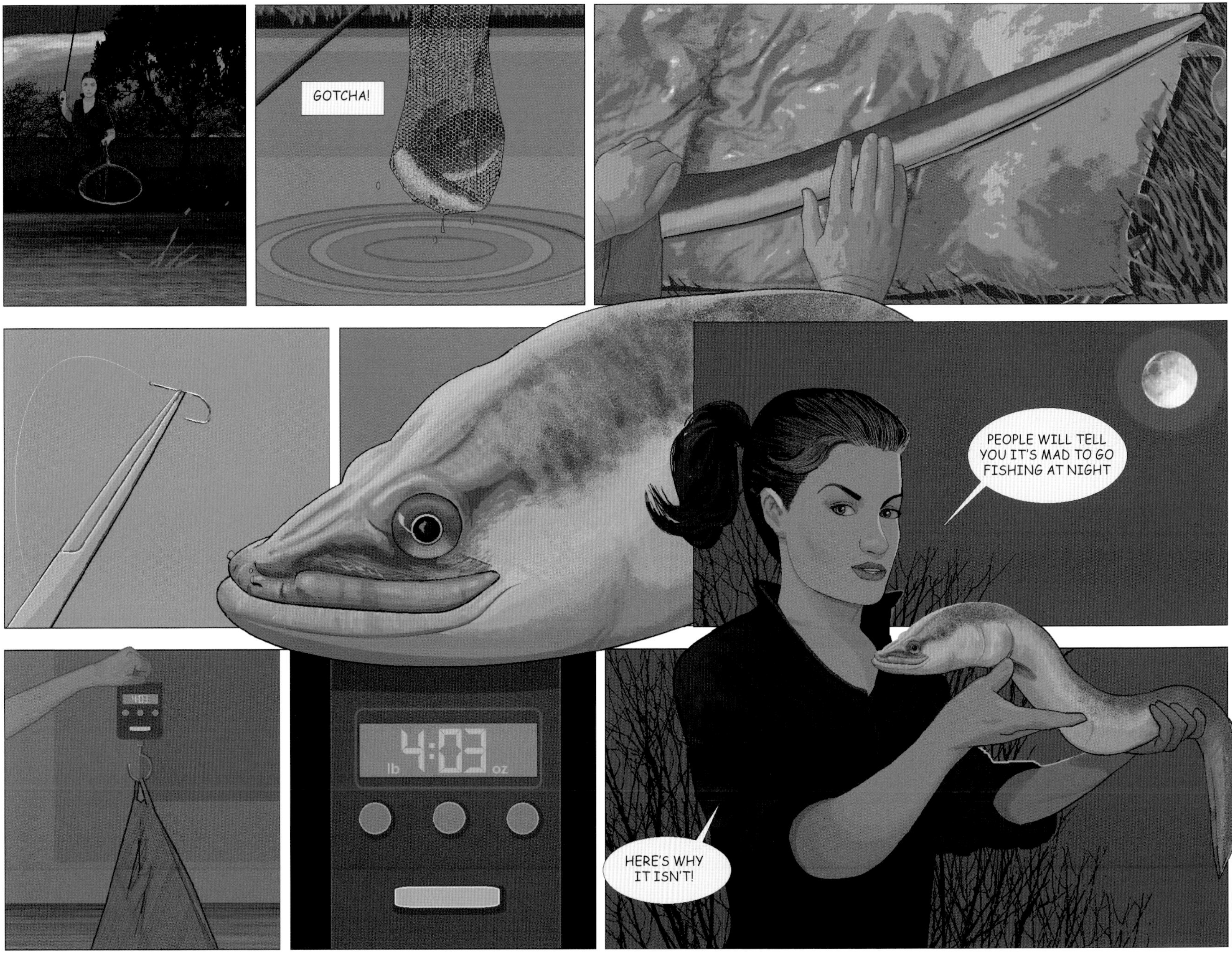
GOTCHA!
4:03 lb oz
PEOPLE WILL TELL YOU IT'S MAD TO GO FISHING AT NIGHT
HERE'S WHY IT ISN'T!

12. Emma on the Edge
Carp from the margins

A Puddlechucker is basically a Waggler but today, rather than just fixing it bottom end only, Emma's banded it to the line. A weighted float like this would normally have a few No. 6 shot added, to get the best presentation but in this case it's just a float and a hook.

The reason is that presentation and even choice of bait is less important than the way the angler approaches the fish and the swim and the main requirement of the rig is that it is as robust as possible.

Carp frequently come in close to the bank. They are cautious because they know that here they are vulnerable but if Emma stays quiet and does nothing to alert the fish to her presence then the results can be amazing. Not many anglers fish the margins.

A Carp hooked in the margins will charge out towards deeper water, crashing through plants and snags as it goes. A float attached bottom end only will soon get wrecked or lost so Emma keeps everything as simple as possible. The float is banded to the line where it will stay put during the fight but allows Emma to alter the depth at which she fishes with ease.

Emma finds that worms in particular are excellent bait for this style of fishing but she's also had success with bread (flake) and even slugs, usually associated with Chub and ghastly to put on the hook, but in some fisheries a slug in the margins can be deadly for Carp.

This type of fishing is real heart-in-the-mouth stuff. A fish feeding virtually under the

WANNA SEE A REALLY SIMPLE RIG?

WELL THEY DON'T GET MORE BASIC THAN THIS - A FLOAT BAND, A PUDDLECHUCKER AND A HOOK

BAIT CAN BE A BUNCH OF MAGGOTS, A PELLET, A LOBWORM

OR EVEN A PIECE OF BREAD OR A SLUG

LET ME SHOW YOU WHY

54

rod tip will often have hooked itself before you've even realised that the float's gone. The first thing that you're aware of is a screaming reel and a rod which, if you're not gripping it, will be trying to follow the fish to the centre of the lake.

Emma begins by wandering around the lake and using her eyes. Most of the anglers present are on the far bank (where the wind on their back is more comfortable) but the fish are showing on the near bank where they've followed the wind and are feeding in the margins. Clouds of mud rise and colour the water as rafts of bubbles agitate the surface.

Emma creeps towards some reeds and quietly lowers the bait into the water. It is vital that the fish don't realise that she's there as they're literally a few feet away.

Once she's got herself and the bait in position, it's simply a matter of waiting quietly.

The higher than normal float is less likely to be pulled under by fish movement and line bites. If it disappears then it's a fish. Her rod is the Pellet Waggler rod again as its softish action will cushion the barbless hook during the ferocious first run of the Carp. It's important to use a reel with a really good clutch, correctly set at the outset.

The screaming run of a Carp exploding out of the margins really must be experienced to be appreciated.

Emma's Carp is a good size. It takes her bait with such confidence that it's hooked by pulling the line tight against the adjacent rod – then the battle begins.

NOW WE WAIT

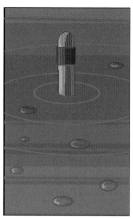

WHOA! DIDN'T EVEN SEE THE FLOAT GO – FISH ON!

THIS FISH IS REALLY MOTORING – IT'S STRONG!

THE CARP BATTLES AWAY FOR TEN MINUTES OR SO UNTIL FINALLY...

AT LAST! FINALLY HE'S TIRING

DO YOU WANT A HAND WITH THE NET?

I'M FINE THANKS – I'VE NETTED HUNDREDS OF THESE

THERE YOU GO: A FEW OUNCES OFF 20LB – A REAL OLD WARRIOR OF A MIRROR CARP

CAUGHT A FOOT OR SO FROM THE BANK ON THE SIMPLEST RIG YOU'LL EVER USE

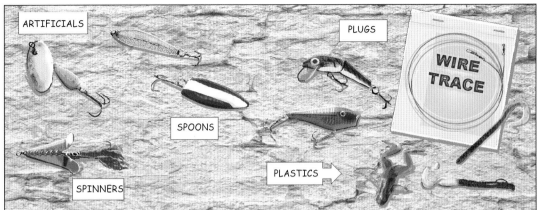

13. Emma in a spin

In 1963 the silver fish living in the Great Ouse Relief Channel got something else to have nightmares about. Pike and Perch were bad enough but all of a sudden a new predator appeared, a fish that seemed to be a combination of both of them.

The Zander was introduced by the Great Ouse River Authority. Its other name – 'Pike-Perch' – is inaccurate, as it's not a hybrid but this name does give a good idea of what the fish looks like. The Zander is long and lean like a Pike but it has the spiny first Dorsal fin of the Perch.

Like the Perch, the Zander has excellent eyesight, especially in low light levels and its huge glassy eyes are one of the first things you notice. That and its teeth, two vampire-like fangs in the front of the upper and lower jaw. These teeth slot into holes in the opposite jaw when the fish closes its mouth.

The technique Emma is going to use to capture one of these striking creatures, is Spinning. As she says, Deadbaiting might be the more obvious tactic (Zander are scavengers as much as predators) but spinning is more active and will allow her to cover a larger area.

She's been in Norfolk all day on business but has a free evening before she drives back home and this Drain has produced many Zander (and Pike) for her in the past. When the Zander was introduced, many feared that the pack-hunting Zander would displace the solitary Pike but this wasn't what happened. It is true that a large Zander can and often does take a small Pike but it's equally true that a large Pike will take a small Zander. And both predators will take fish of their own species. What usually happens when Pike and Zander are in the same waterway, is that the Zander hunt in the deeper, darker stretches whilst the Pike stick to ambushing from the clearer shallows.

Lure fishing is a big topic. The range of Lures currently available is greater than ever. New materials and modern production have spawned a bewildering number of styles, types and patterns that can leave the newcomer at a loss where to start.

Broadly speaking they can be split into Spinners, Spoons, Plugs and Plastics. The illustration on the previous page will give you a bit of an idea but each category can then be split even further. Take Plugs for example: the body can be one piece or jointed two, three or more times. There are Floating Plugs, Sinking Plugs, Poppers, Crawlers, Rattling Plugs, Diving Plugs (which can be adjusted to dive to different depths).

Tonight though Emma chooses a Spinner of a pattern that's been around for years. It's a small Spinner she often uses for Perch and she's added some red wool to the hooks (Perch are drawn to the colour red).

She also periodically sprays it with WD40 which keeps the lure working well and is thought by many anglers to be a draw to predators. The small lure is the right size for Zander which don't have large mouths but to induce a bite Emma is going to have to make the lure work.

The Spinner will, obviously, spin but in the right hands it can do a lot more than that. The idea with a lure is to convince the predator that it is not only a fish but an injured fish. Predators keep the water healthy and they prey on the sick and injured. They're not usually inclined to chase a fit and healthy fish around: they want an easy meal.

If the lure already looks like a fish and in addition, moves like an injured fish, the illusion is complete and results should follow.

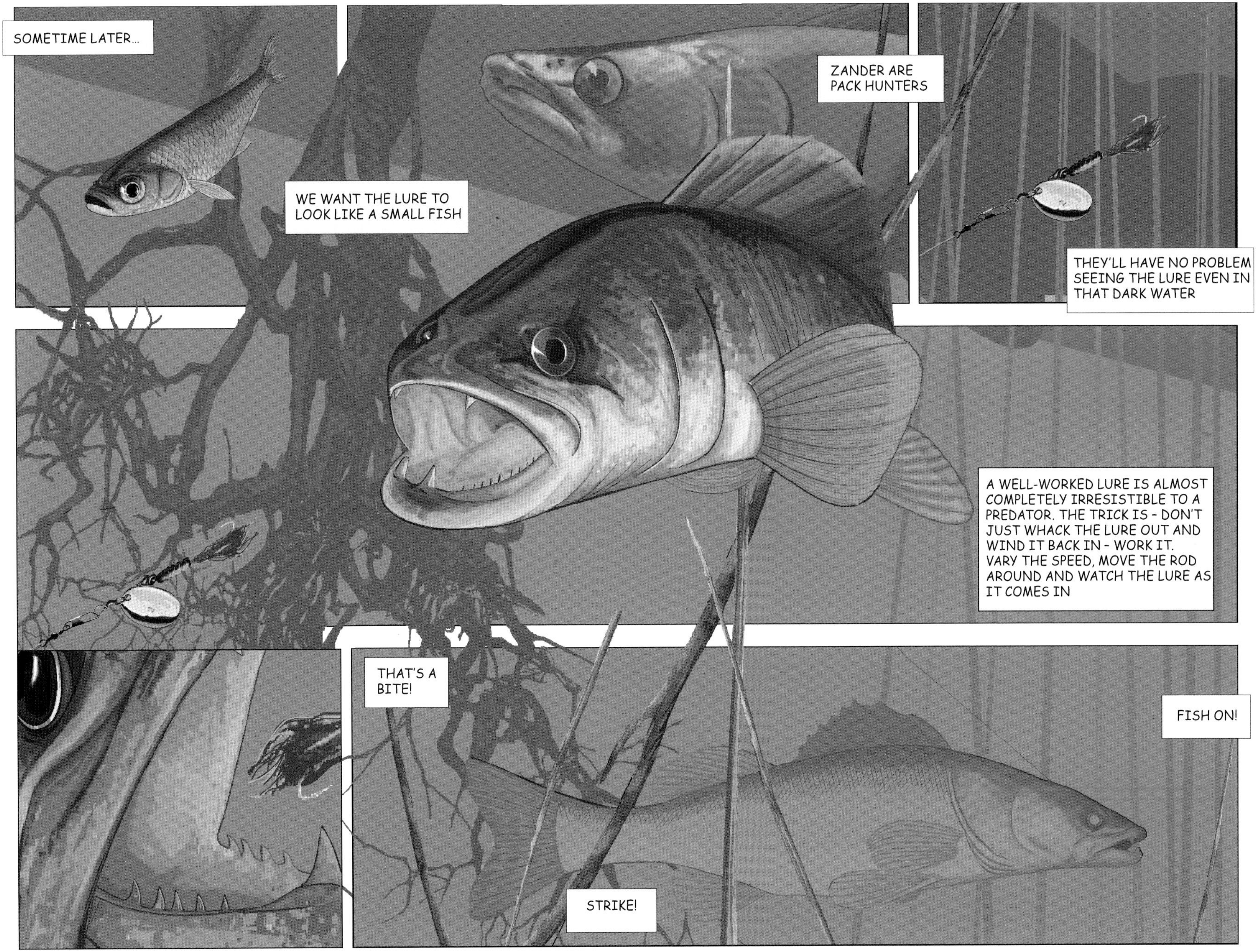
SOMETIME LATER...
WE WANT THE LURE TO LOOK LIKE A SMALL FISH
ZANDER ARE PACK HUNTERS
THEY'LL HAVE NO PROBLEM SEEING THE LURE EVEN IN THAT DARK WATER
A WELL-WORKED LURE IS ALMOST COMPLETELY IRRESISTIBLE TO A PREDATOR. THE TRICK IS - DON'T JUST WHACK THE LURE OUT AND WIND IT BACK IN - WORK IT. VARY THE SPEED, MOVE THE ROD AROUND AND WATCH THE LURE AS IT COMES IN
THAT'S A BITE!
STRIKE!
FISH ON!

COME TO MOMMA!

THERE HE IS

YOU CAN SEE WHY I USE FORCEPS

LOOK AT THOSE TEETH!

LET'S SLIP HIM BACK SO WE CAN CATCH HIM AGAIN IN A FEW YEARS WHEN HE'S A BIT BIGGER

Emma watches the lure carefully as she retrieves it. Predators often follow a lure right up to the bank but it's also by watching the lure that you learn how to make it work in the water, by varying the speed as you move the rod. The angler brings life to the lure but it takes practice.

Emma's fishing in the evening as the light begins to fade. Early in the morning or late evening, the first or last hour of daylight is often the best time to catch fish and Zander in particular are more active in low light.

She's using a head torch not because she intends fishing on into complete darkness but purely for safety.

Handling an irate toothy predator with a treble hook somewhere in its mouth in dull light needs to be done carefully.

The light from the head torch makes the whole operation a lot safer but even so, Emma uses a pair of long-nosed forceps and ensures she has a secure hold on the fish.

The treble hooks on the Spinner have had their barbs crushed with a strong pair of pliers to render them barbless (Emma does a lot of coaching and barbed hooks and youngsters are not a good mix). This also makes the unhooking procedure a lot easier and safer.

Zander, like Pike, are fierce-looking predators but also both species need to be handled carefully and returned as soon as possible.

14. Emma's on a Roll
Rolling leger and Static feeder for Barbel

The Barbel is a long muscular river fish with large fins and a flattened belly. Its torpedo shape is appropriate because that's what you'll feel you're attached to when you hook one. They are an extremely popular and respected sport fish that make for a powerful and demanding quarry.

Will has yet to encounter one of these but is in safe hands with Emma as she's had many battles with these beautiful creatures.

She's given Will the best spot, opposite a raft of floating duckweed and twigs across the far bank.

Their rods are strong enough to deal with the quarry and the conditions, reels are robust and importantly both have an excellent clutch. Line is 10lb for Will and 8lb for Emma. Hooks are a strong size 6.

Will's fishing a cage feeder. He plugs one end with Groundbait, fills it with pellets and then seals them in with more Groundbait pushed into the other end.

He doesn't want to make too many casts as he could spook the fish, so once his rig is in place, he uses a catapult to fire in additional free pellets.

61

FIRST THINGS FIRST.
BARBEL ARE THE MOST
POWERFUL COARSE
RIVER FISH

THEY FIGHT LONG AND
HARD AND NEVER GIVE
UP – HOOK ONE OF THESE
BOYS AND YOU'LL KNOW IT!

ON A BRIGHT DAY LIKE
TODAY THEY'LL TAKE
ADVANTAGE OF ANY COVER
WHICH IS WHY THAT RAFT
IS IDEAL

Emma's staying mobile today. She's left Will in the best spot, opposite that raft and she won't stray too far from him. But a roving approach will allow her to explore the river around Will's position.

In contrast to Will who's using a modern method, Emma's using a much older technique: that of Rolling leger. She knows this stretch of river well and it's not snaggy so she's using a drilled bullet weight. If it was snaggy, or she was less sure of the swim then she'd switch to a Link leger.

There are two advantages to Link leger: firstly the number of Swan shot can easily be adjusted until you get the weight just right. Too heavy, just pull off one of the Swan shot, too light, just pinch on another.

Secondly if the weight gets caught in a snag on the river bottom, you won't lose your whole rig. A firm tug on the rod and the Shot will be left in the snag whilst the remainder of the rig can be wound back in.

With a Rolling leger you want the weight to just hold the bottom. As the pressure of the current builds up, the weight is dragged a little way downstream. Here it holds the bottom again until the build up of pressure drags it downstream a little further. In

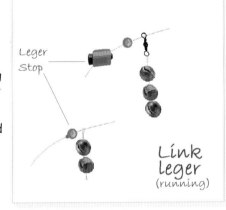

this way Emma can explore a large area of water and is also able to let her bait roll into spots that it would be hard to cast to directly.

She's Touch legering, that is, feeling for bites. This simple and direct method combined with the speed and power of her quarry make for extremely exciting fishing.

You'll notice she's taking great care returning her Barbel. This is especially important with this species. Barbel are hard fighting fish and as a consequence are often exhausted once you get them on the bank.

If Barbel are just 'dropped' back in, they can be carried downstream, unable to right themselves in the current where they will drown.

To avoid this, simply position the fish back in the water with its head pointing upstream, allowing oxygenated water to flow back over its gills.

The fish can be held gently in the hands while it is returned, as Emma's doing, or in a landing net. Allow the fish time to regain its strength. Then Emma removes her one hand from under the Barbel's chin and just keeps hold of its tail, waiting until the fish is strong enough to kick away from her grip.

Also remember: the longer the Barbel is out of the water, the longer the recovery time will be.

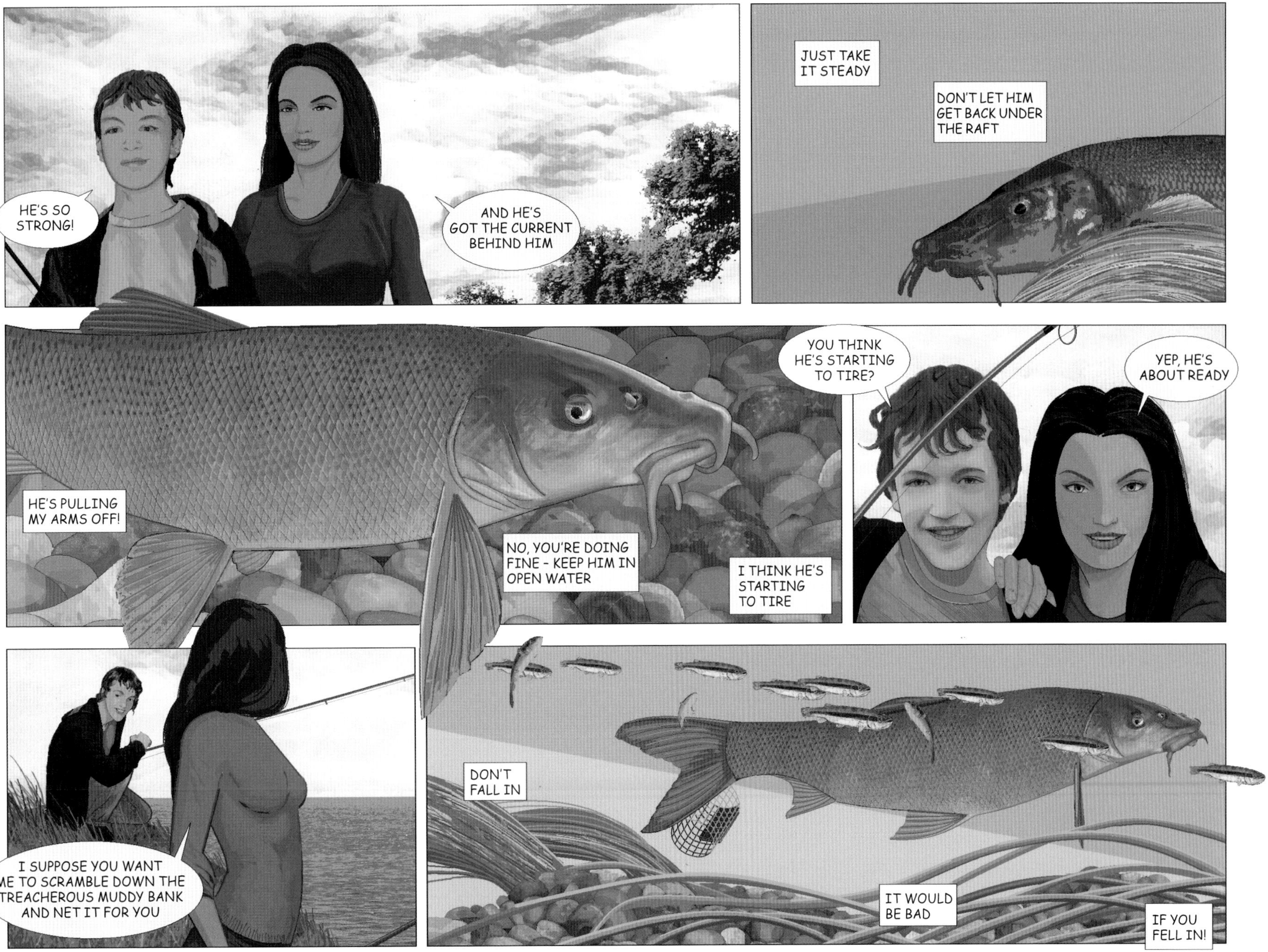
HE'S SO STRONG!
AND HE'S GOT THE CURRENT BEHIND HIM
JUST TAKE IT STEADY
DON'T LET HIM GET BACK UNDER THE RAFT
HE'S PULLING MY ARMS OFF!
NO, YOU'RE DOING FINE - KEEP HIM IN OPEN WATER
I THINK HE'S STARTING TO TIRE
YOU THINK HE'S STARTING TO TIRE?
YEP, HE'S ABOUT READY
I SUPPOSE YOU WANT ME TO SCRAMBLE DOWN THE TREACHEROUS MUDDY BANK AND NET IT FOR YOU
DON'T FALL IN
IT WOULD BE BAD
IF YOU FELL IN!

Will meanwhile has been patiently waiting for the trail of freebies from his feeder to draw a Barbel out from under the raft to his hookbait.

He's fishing with a Feeder rod and has the rod tip high off the rest to keep his line off the water.

The bite when it comes is a real wrench, as Barbel bites can be (they can just as often be a few gentle taps as well). Which is why you should always be near your rod.

Will's caught a few double figure Carp in his time but a big Barbel in a powerful river is going to be an experience that he'll always remember.

The trick is not to try and net it too soon. Many a 'beaten' Barbel can manage another scorching run when it sees the landing net.

Small Barbel or big Gudgeon?

The easiest and most reliable way of telling these two species apart is to count the barbules

2 and it's a Gudgeon

4 and it's a Barbel

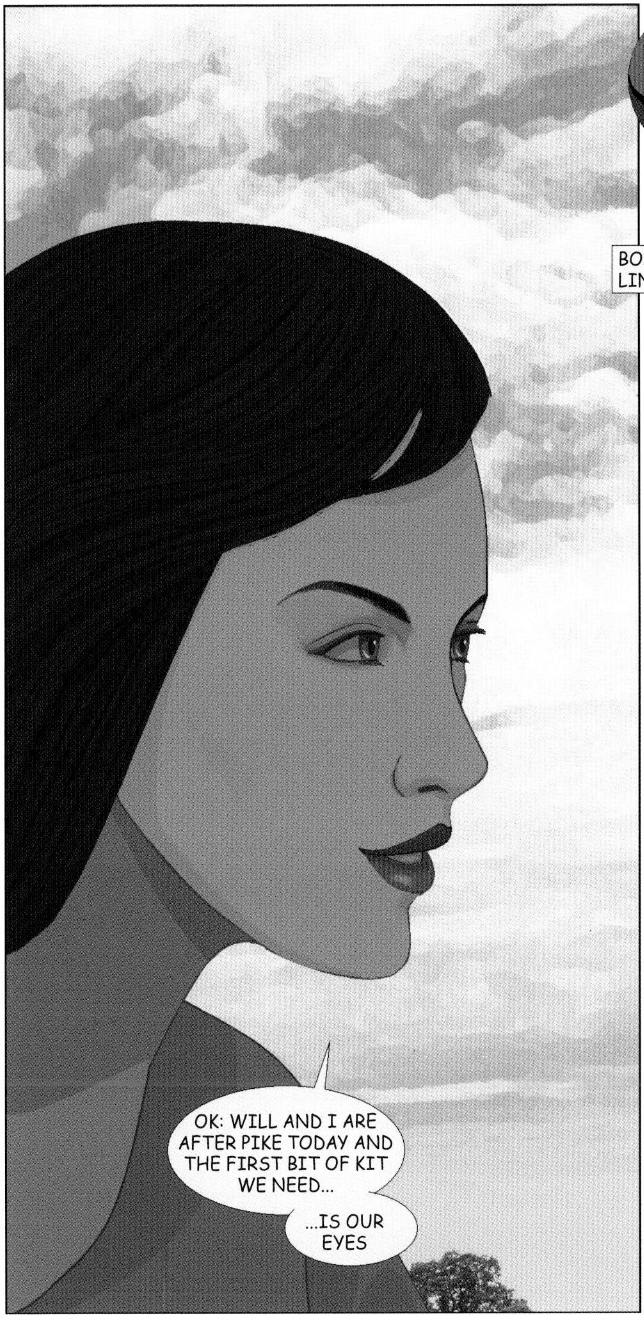

OK: WILL AND I ARE AFTER PIKE TODAY AND THE FIRST BIT OF KIT WE NEED...
...IS OUR EYES

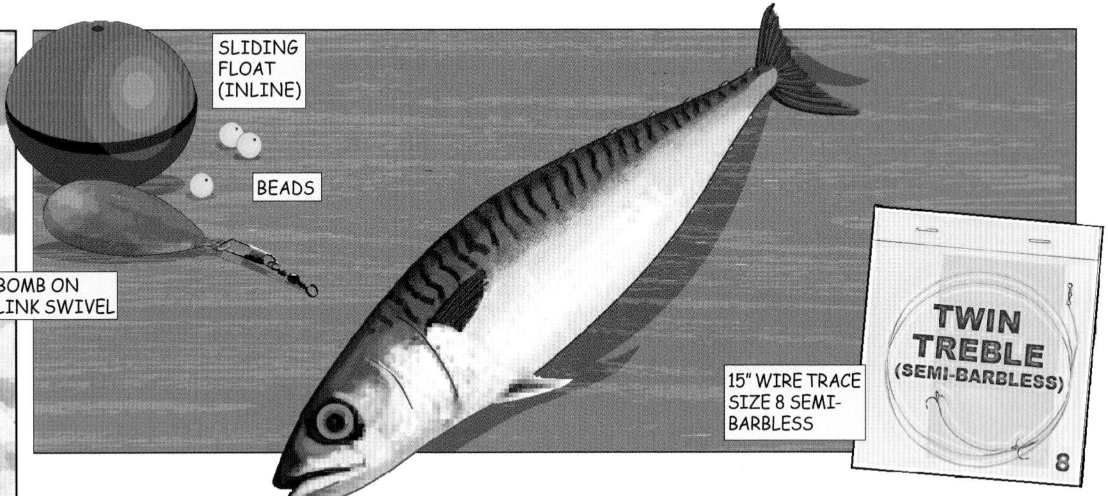

SLIDING FLOAT (INLINE)
BEADS
BOMB ON LINK SWIVEL
15" WIRE TRACE SIZE 8 SEMI-BARBLESS
TWIN TREBLE (SEMI-BARBLESS)
8

15. A Mackerel to catch a Pike

Today Emma's after Pike. There's more myths, more scare stories, more 'one that got away' tales, more mis-information about Pike than any other Coarse species. This is a fish with a reputation, a dodgy past, a fish with bad press. A freshwater Shark, the merciless killer of anything that ventures into its watery domain. No fish, duck or stick-fetching dog is safe. Truth is of course they just do what they do. A predator obviously (just look at that mouth) but a monster? Well they can get big but stick-fetching dogs can sleep soundly (probably).

Fishing in Wales as a boy, fishery rules told me that any Pike I caught had to be killed but it was whilst fishing a farm pond on holiday in Ireland that I first encountered *Esox lucius*. He wasn't a monster (that was my second one!) but he was the most beautiful fish I'd ever seen. Beautiful might seem an odd word to use but you must remember that only the fisherman sees the true colour of a fish. In tanks, or dead on a fishmonger's slab, fish colours are muted, faded, washed out in comparison to those of the living fish just out of the water. Talk to any Aquarist and they'll tell you that fish that appear colourful in a tank, are even more so in the net when lifted out of the water.

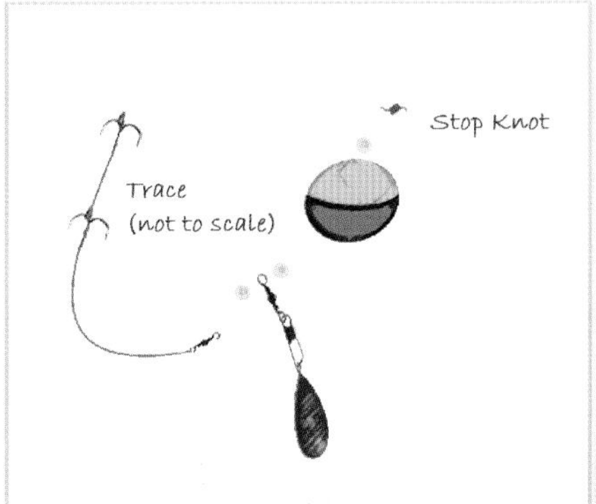

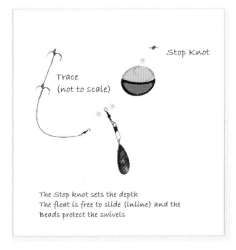

Stop Knot
Trace
(not to scale)

The Stop knot sets the depth
The float is free to slide (inline) and the
Beads protect the swivels

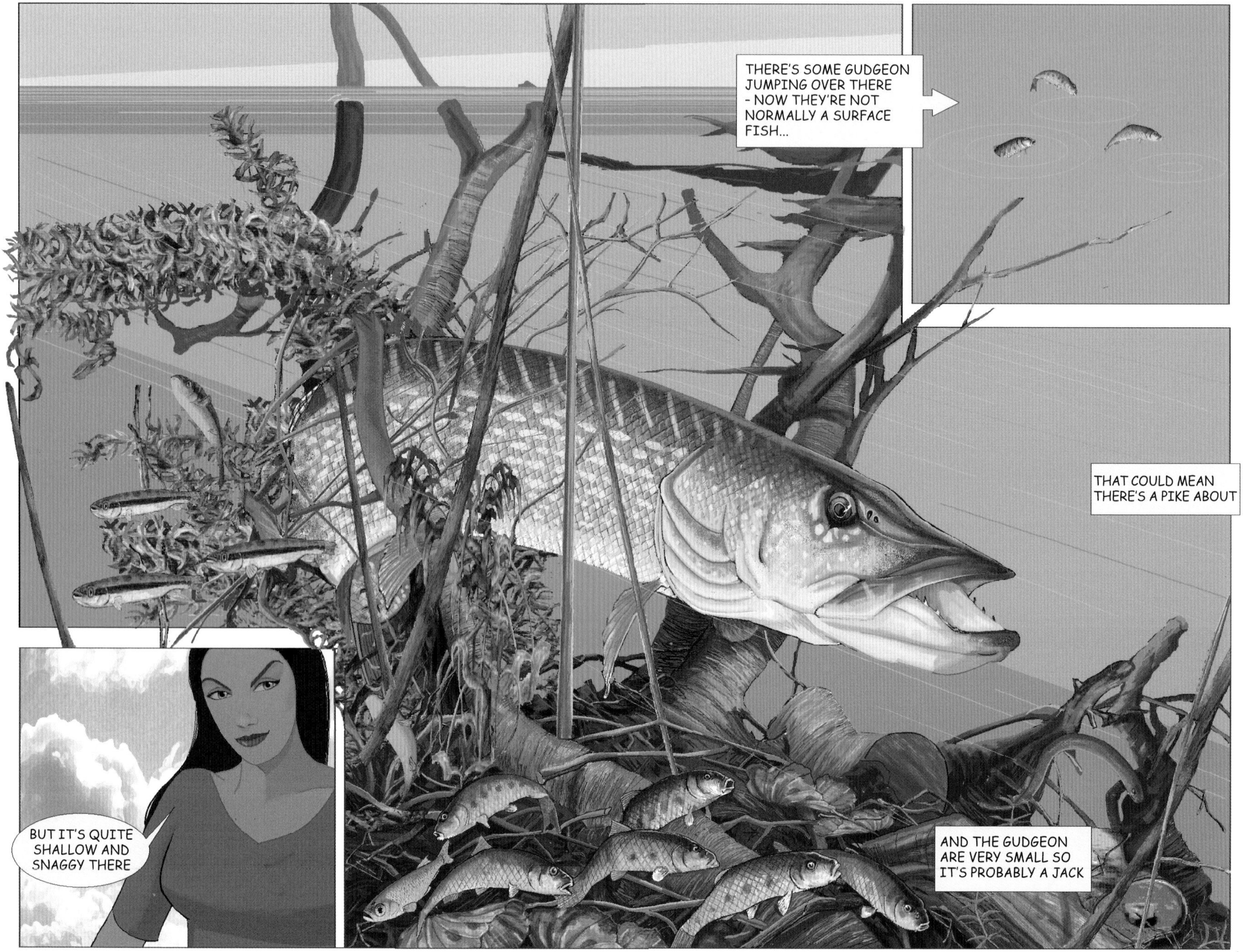
THERE'S SOME GUDGEON JUMPING OVER THERE - NOW THEY'RE NOT NORMALLY A SURFACE FISH...
THAT COULD MEAN THERE'S A PIKE ABOUT
BUT IT'S QUITE SHALLOW AND SNAGGY THERE
AND THE GUDGEON ARE VERY SMALL SO IT'S PROBABLY A JACK

FLOAT IS FREE TO SLIDE UP THE LINE UNTIL IT REACHES THE STOP KNOT

THERE'S A GOOD-LOOKING SHELTERED BAY OVER THERE. IT'S GOT A REED BED BEHIND IT AND I'VE HAD PIKE FROM THERE BEFORE

IT'S AROUND FIVE FEET DEEP – SO WE SLIDE THE STOP KNOT UP TO GIVE US THAT DEPTH AND LOB IT OUT

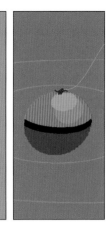

NOW WE WATCH

AND WE WAIT

Pike are truly stunning. A network of intricate and delicate patterns and colours cover the body of what is clearly a predator. For an illustrator they're a real headache. Sure, it's easy enough to capture the look of the fish but the true colour and texture are another matter entirely. Pinks, blues, purples, turquoise and gold are all there when you hold a freshly caught Pike and it's holding this fish safely that we'll be looking at in this chapter.

But before she can show Will how to handle Pike on the bank, Emma has to catch one. She looks for signs that a Pike might be hunting, or for places that might conceal one that's waiting for a meal.

The Pike is an ambush predator: a long lean body and a fin area at the rear which is all about one thing – blistering acceleration. Pike don't chase their prey around, they hide and they wait, then when the prey is close enough, they burst from cover and strike.

So why is Emma using a dead Mackerel (a sea fish) to catch a fresh-water ambush predator? Well, we mentioned that in the past Pike had to be killed: this policy once used to be quite common but nowadays, thankfully, it has disappeared and for one very simple reason. It never worked! The policy was intended to protect fisheries and fish stocks but removing the Pike in the long-run made matters worse. Put simply: Nature knows best. The predators take out the sick, injured and diseased (the easiest to catch) and keep the fish population at a viable level. Without Pike, thousands of stunted fish can become a breeding ground for bacterial and parasitic infections.

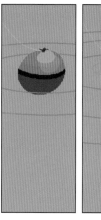

And it's the Pike's role as remover of the dead or dying that we can exploit by using deadbaits.

Emma's using a sea deadbait because they work (there are problems with Coarse fish deadbaits which we'll look at later) and because they're easy to get hold of. Sea deads don't work for all freshwater predators but they do for Pike. Mackerel, Herring, Sprat and Smelt are favourites. Emma's gone for Mackerel because their skin is very tough (less likely to fly off the hooks on the cast) and they're extremely oily so their scent trail carries a long way in the water.

She's also been able to get hold of some fairly small Mackerel from her local supermarket (if they're too large they can be cut in half). The rig she's using relies on a float for bite indication and a Leger for distance and

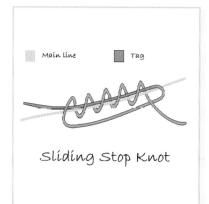

Sliding Stop Knot

getting the bait down. The float slides on the line and relies on a stop knot to set the depth.

Emma watches Will and as soon as the float starts to run she tells him to strike.

When you're starting out with Pike, it's a good idea to strike early as it's better to lose the odd fish than have a deeply hooked one to contend with. Pike can swallow their prey really

70

quickly and you don't want your hooks in their stomach. Will picks up the rod and starts to wind in. The second he feels the weight of the fish he strikes and the fish is hooked.

Pike fights are often long and can be spectacular with the fish jumping clear of the water. Will's fish runs him around for a bit shaking its head then abruptly it just gives in to the inevitable. Emma slides the net under it and then things get interesting. Catching Pike is one thing, unhooking them is another. Without doubt the best advice for any wannabe Pike angler is to begin by fishing with somebody who knows what they're doing and is experienced in handling Pike out of the water.

The first problem is that Pike aren't as strong as they look and they mustn't be out of the water for too long. The second problem is a that

a Pike's mouth is a dangerous place to be. There are teeth everywhere and even the edge of the gill rakers can give you a nasty gash.

In his book *Tench: How to catch them* Harry Brotherton pointed to the success of the Carp-Catchers Club as an example of experienced anglers getting together to pool information. That was in 1954 and today there are groups for all of the major species. When Pike anglers got together they soon came up with a reliable procedure for handling and unhooking Pike that's safe for both you and the fish.

Emma lies the Pike on its back on the unhooking mat and carefully slides her fingers under the gill cover. If the hooks are in the back of the Pike's mouth, make sure you don't push your fingers into them.

THIS WAY WE CAN KEEP THE FISH UNDER CONTROL

- AND GET HER BACK IN THE WATER WITHOUT DELAY

THE TRICK TO HANDLING PIKE – OR ANY FISH – OUT OF THE WATER IS CONFIDENCE. THE FISH SEEM TO SENSE YOUR CONFIDENCE AND ARE LESS INCLINED TO FLAP ABOUT. LOOK AT THE ILLUSTRATION OF THE INSIDE OF A PIKE'S MOUTH. IT'S SIMPLIFIED BUT GIVES AN IDEA OF THE LAYOUT. PIKE ARE DESIGNED TO GET FOOD FROM MOUTH TO STOMACH REALLY QUICKLY – IF WE STRIKE THE BITE QUICKLY WE KEEP THE HOOKS IN THE FRONT OF THE MOUTH. IF THE HOOKS ARE FURTHER BACK IT'S POSSIBLE TO GET FORCEPS BEHIND THE GILL COVERS BUT IT MUST BE DONE WITH CARE

STOMACH OPENING

GILL RAKERS

REMEMBER WE WANT TO RETURN THESE FISH IN THE CONDITION THAT WE FOUND THEM

She keeps the Pike still with gentle pressure from her knees and once her fingers are in place inside the gill cover she is able to grip it and lift the fish. She can keep the Pike's mouth open in this way and can use long nosed-forceps in her other hand to remove the hooks. It looks a cruel way to handle a fish but in truth it's the best and safest method. The hooks are semi-barbless trebles, which means one hook is barbed (this is the one that goes into and holds onto the deadbait) and the other two are barbless, which means they can be removed easily from the Pike's mouth.

The other thing to notice about the rig is the wire trace, a 15" length of wire that the Pike can't bite through (unlike Mono). You must use a wire trace for Pike.

Of course it's one thing to read about handling Pike out of the water: it's quite a different matter when you're the one with a large irate Pike on the bank that needs you to remove a set of hooks from inside its mouth.

The best answer is, as we've said, to start by Pike fishing with someone who's done it all before. If you don't know anyone, ask at your local tackle shop or approach one of the groups that specialise in Pike.

The internet has facilitated sharing know-how and most fishing groups are easy to contact and only too willing to help.

16. Emma and the big Cat
(or raining cats and spods)

So there I was, pond I've never seen before, hammering down with rain, three hours of nothing then out of nowhere, I get a run that nearly drags the rod in and I'm hanging on for dear life!

I found a nice gravel bar about fifty yards out and spodded out a load of Halibut pellets. A Spod is a baiting rocket. You can fill it with pellets or Boilies or Groundbait and simply cast it out to the area you're fishing and each cast puts out a bed of bait. This Fishery is one rod only but you're allowed a spare, so you can set up a second rod with a Spod or Marker float to prepare your area and keep it topped up with freebies.

I put some pellets on a hair with superglue. I simply cut them in half, added a drop of glue and sandwiched the hair between the two halves. I've used two pellets at an angle to each other to make them harder for the Carp to eject.

I used a Fixed rig or Bolt rig with the lead secured by a safety clip and in all honesty I just banged it out there and hoped for the best.

One of the biggest problems with many Commercial fisheries nowadays is the lack of variety. Often you pretty much know what you're going to catch before you turn up and it's just a question of numbers. Surprises can be few and far between so days like today become extra special.

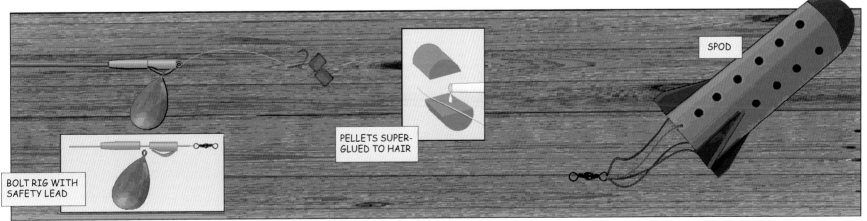

73

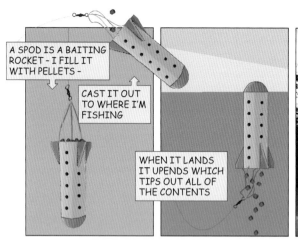

A SPOD IS A BAITING ROCKET - I FILL IT WITH PELLETS -

CAST IT OUT TO WHERE I'M FISHING

WHEN IT LANDS IT UPENDS WHICH TIPS OUT ALL OF THE CONTENTS

I'VE BEEN HERE A FEW HOURS BUT NOTHING'S HAPPENING AND THE WEATHER'S NOT HELPING

THE OTHER ANGLERS HAVE GONE HOME APART FROM GI JOE OVER THERE...

BUT HE HASN'T FOUND THE CARP EITHER

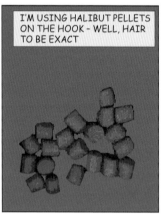

I'M USING HALIBUT PELLETS ON THE HOOK - WELL, HAIR TO BE EXACT

THEIR SMELL WILL DRAW THE CARP

I'VE SPODDED OUT LOADS OF FREEBIES BUT NOTHING'S MOVING

LOOKS LIKE IT'LL BE A QUIET DAY

Despite walking around the lake and spending a lot of time looking, I saw no obvious signs of fish activity except for a large shoal of stunted Rudd. Eventually I settled for a likely-looking area and after exploring it with the marker float, I baited it up.

But it was one of those days, no fish showing, nobody catching, and the weather forecast's prediction of a bright sunny day went more and more wrong.

Light rain turned to drizzle, drizzle turned into a downpour, the bank turned into a wet mud slide and pretty soon most of the other anglers had given up.

I was after a 'Ghostie' or Ghost Carp or Ghost Koi to give them their proper title. Koi are an ornamental variety of King Carp and are a popular choice for large garden ponds. They've started turning up in more and more Commercial fisheries these days. They're exceptionally hard-fighting Carp, lean and muscular – hook one of these and you'll know it. A big pale Ghost Koi is a stunning sight on the bank.

What I didn't know was that there were Catfish in the lake. The European or Wels Catfish was introduced into this country over a hundred years ago and now these fish, like Ghost Koi, are starting to turn up all over.

The thing about Wels is the size that they get. They've been caught, over 100lb in this country and well over 200lb in Europe. If you're after them, it's specialist gear and strong tackle but many anglers, like me, run into them whilst they're chasing Carp and when this happens, believe me, you're in for the fight of your life!

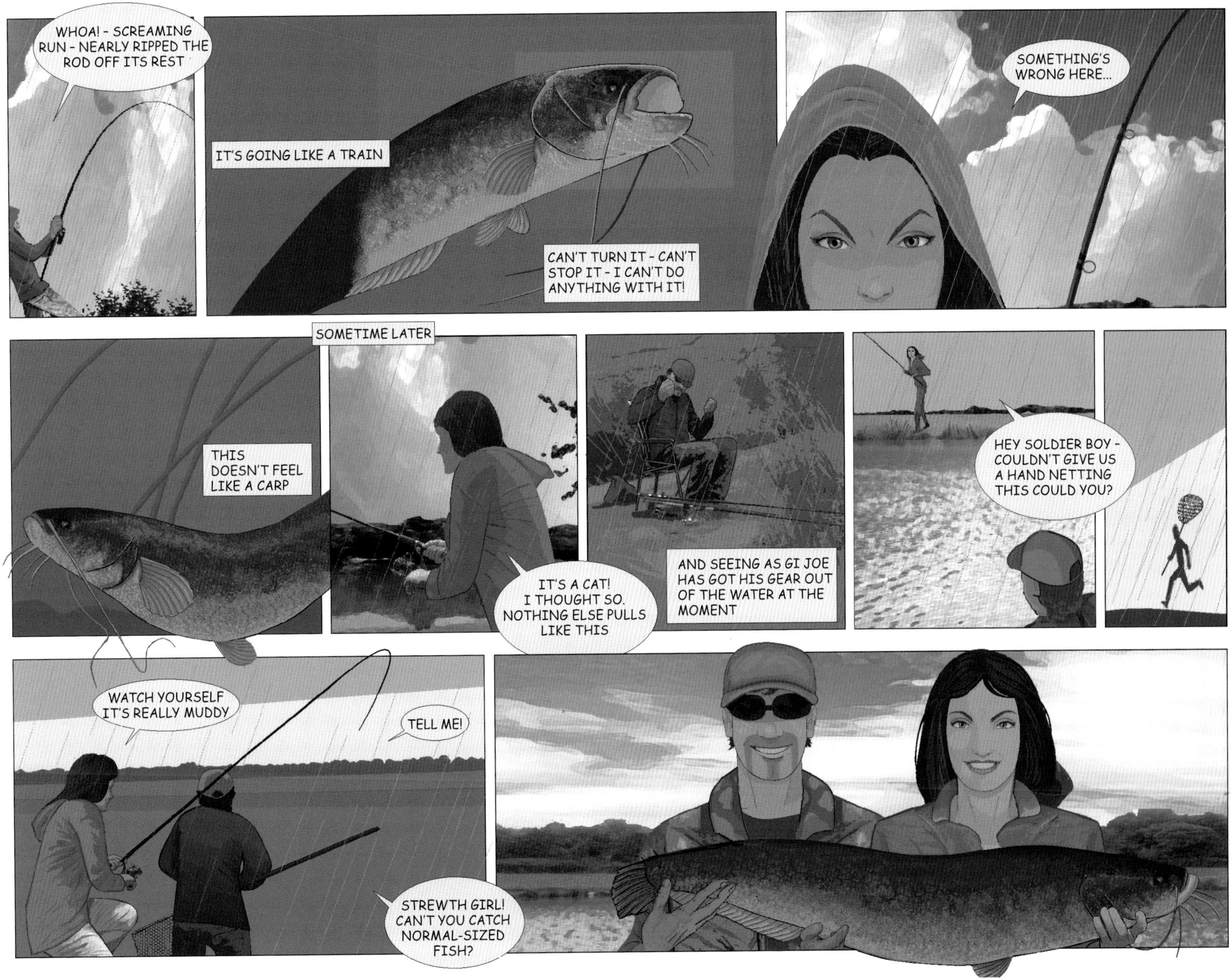
WHOA! - SCREAMING RUN - NEARLY RIPPED THE ROD OFF ITS REST
IT'S GOING LIKE A TRAIN
CAN'T TURN IT - CAN'T STOP IT - I CAN'T DO ANYTHING WITH IT!
SOMETHING'S WRONG HERE...
THIS DOESN'T FEEL LIKE A CARP
SOMETIME LATER
IT'S A CAT! I THOUGHT SO. NOTHING ELSE PULLS LIKE THIS
AND SEEING AS GI JOE HAS GOT HIS GEAR OUT OF THE WATER AT THE MOMENT
HEY SOLDIER BOY - COULDN'T GIVE US A HAND NETTING THIS COULD YOU?
WATCH YOURSELF IT'S REALLY MUDDY
TELL ME!
STREWTH GIRL! CAN'T YOU CATCH NORMAL-SIZED FISH?

17. Emma's Bad Day

Matt Hayes, genius angler and communicator (and a fan of Chub) memorably described them as 'real dirty fighters' and anyone who's tangled with these powerful, cunning fish will know exactly what he means. A hooked Chub knows the location of every available snag in the surrounding area and will immediately bolt for the nearest. Given half a chance they'll wrap your line (and themselves) around the nearest submerged branch or tree root, or roll their mouth across a reed stem and in doing so, transfer the hook from their mouth to the plant. Many an angler has gone from playing a lively Chub to wrestling with submerged undergrowth with no idea how the fish achieved it. Fishing for Chub can be a humbling experience.

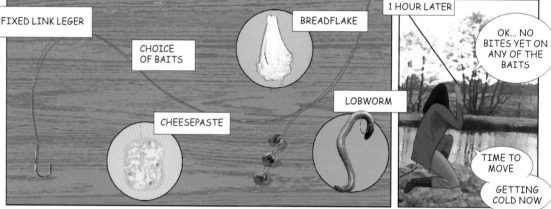

Primarily a river fish (although they're becoming more common in stillwaters) like many of our Coarse species the young fish are much easier to catch than the adults. They're not fussy feeders. Worms, maggots, slugs, bread, cheese, pellets and even small deadbaits will succeed if the fish is in the mood and the angler does nothing to spook the fish.

Take a look at the illustration of Emma's rig. This is the Link leger we mentioned earlier but set up in a slightly different way.

Emma's using six pound line straight through to a No. 8 barbless hook. Instead of a Sliding link leger, the shorter length of line that bears the shot has been tied directly to the main line by means of a four turn water knot *(see page 38)*. Onto this have been squeezed several large shot (again, just enough to hold bottom).

Although this is now a fixed rig it still has the advantages of being easy to adjust (by adding or removing shot) and easy to pull free if it snags.

One of the things that we wanted to show you with this book is that a day's fishing doesn't always go as planned. Some anglers claim that they need only turn up at a lake or river and anything with gills and fins will throw itself into the nearest landing net.

The truth is that there will be red letter days but there will also be the dreaded blanks days when nothing gets caught and nothing goes right.

The problem here is that Emma's heard the weather forecast but hasn't planned accordingly.

It is lovely to be at the waterside in fine weather but sitting for a couple of hours in the cold or wet and wind is a completely different matter.

Now Chub will feed in the cold but generally they need a couple of days to acclimatise. Here Emma arrives as the temperature is rapidly dropping which greatly decreases her chances of catching.

She counters this by using a roving approach, staying mobile, taking a minimum of equipment. The Link leger will allow her to search for the fish and staying mobile will help with the cold but it's going to get really cold.

Nowadays outdoor clothing has become an industry and there is some excellent specialist gear available. The most effective system uses 3 layers. A base layer (next to skin) must insulate and be moisture wicking (drawing moisture away from your skin). The mid layer provides insulation by trapping the warm air around your body, so it needs to fit properly. The outer layer is the thickest and warmest insulating layer like a jacket or heavy fleece.

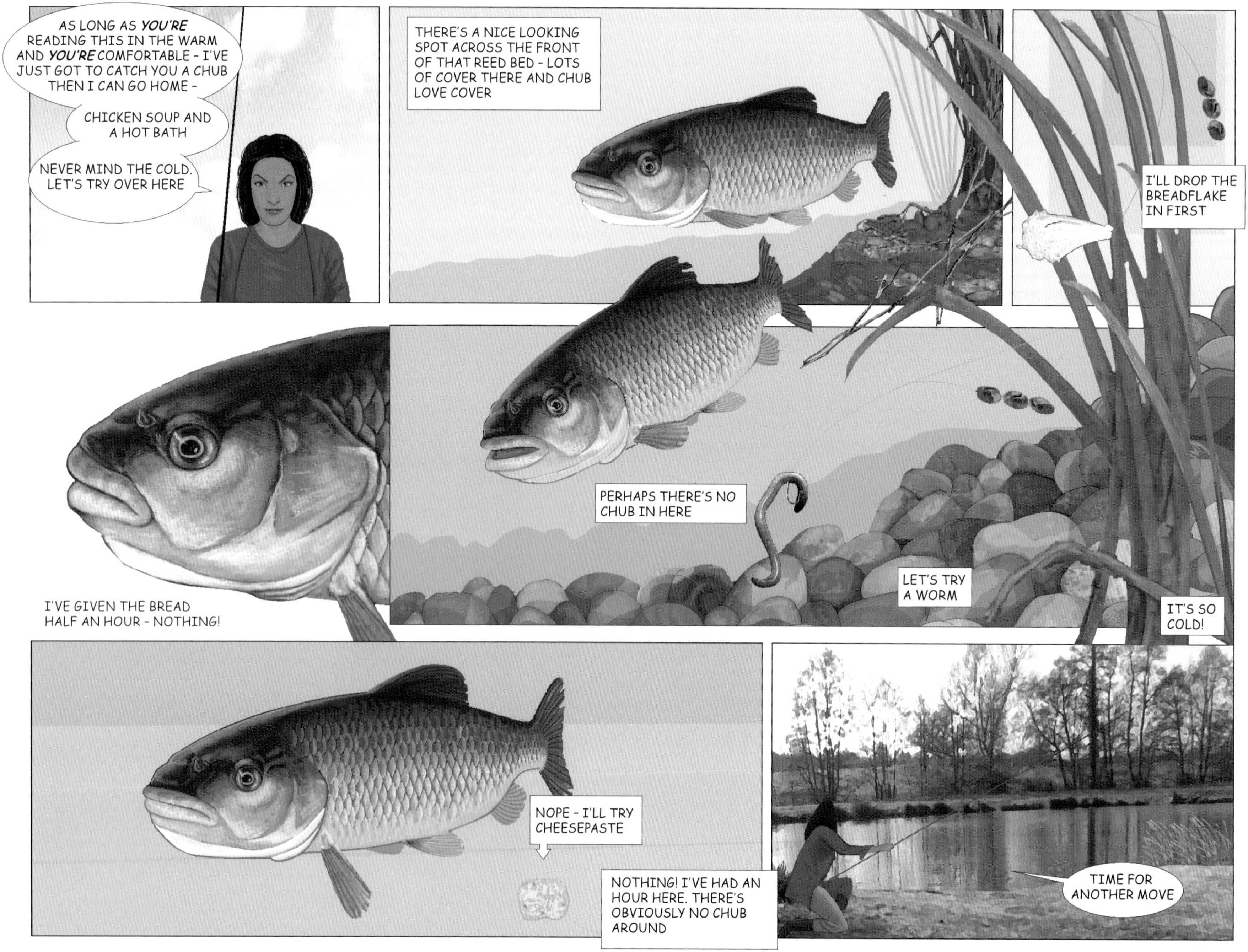
AS LONG AS *YOU'RE* READING THIS IN THE WARM AND *YOU'RE* COMFORTABLE - I'VE JUST GOT TO CATCH YOU A CHUB THEN I CAN GO HOME -
CHICKEN SOUP AND A HOT BATH
NEVER MIND THE COLD. LET'S TRY OVER HERE
THERE'S A NICE LOOKING SPOT ACROSS THE FRONT OF THAT REED BED - LOTS OF COVER THERE AND CHUB LOVE COVER
I'LL DROP THE BREADFLAKE IN FIRST
I'VE GIVEN THE BREAD HALF AN HOUR - NOTHING!
PERHAPS THERE'S NO CHUB IN HERE
LET'S TRY A WORM
IT'S SO COLD!
NOPE - I'LL TRY CHEESEPASTE
NOTHING! I'VE HAD AN HOUR HERE. THERE'S OBVIOUSLY NO CHUB AROUND
TIME FOR ANOTHER MOVE

Water in the wellies is a different matter: we've all done it. As a lad fishing with mates on the banks of the tidal Usk in Newport, one of us, usually me, would often find ourselves sinking in the mud and on finally scrambling out would discover that another welly was gone forever.

Emma on the other hand (and she won't mind me saying this) has been a bit thick! You never step into water if you don't know how deep it is, even if it's an area you think you know well. Remember water levels can change and change quickly. What makes her error worse is that she's carrying a landing net, the handle of which is perfect for checking the depth. All she'd needed to do was just probe ahead of her with the handle before she'd stepped in.

Her final error involves the bank itself. River banks erode over time and you should always be careful if you're near the edge, especially if you're fishing on your own.

The final thing that happens is completely outside her control. The small struggling Chub that she's hooked attracts the attention of another river predator, a Pike. Many anglers have had the experience of winding in one fish to suddenly feel an instant increase in weight and strength and realise that their fish has been grabbed by another.

I have seen a Jack (small Pike) grab a 6oz Rudd that was being brought in. The Jack refused point blank to let go of his meal and the angler landed both. Usually though, both Pike and prey are lost but it's worth reading our section on handling Pike, even if you don't intend fishing for them, as you never know when you'll get an unexpected 'double'!

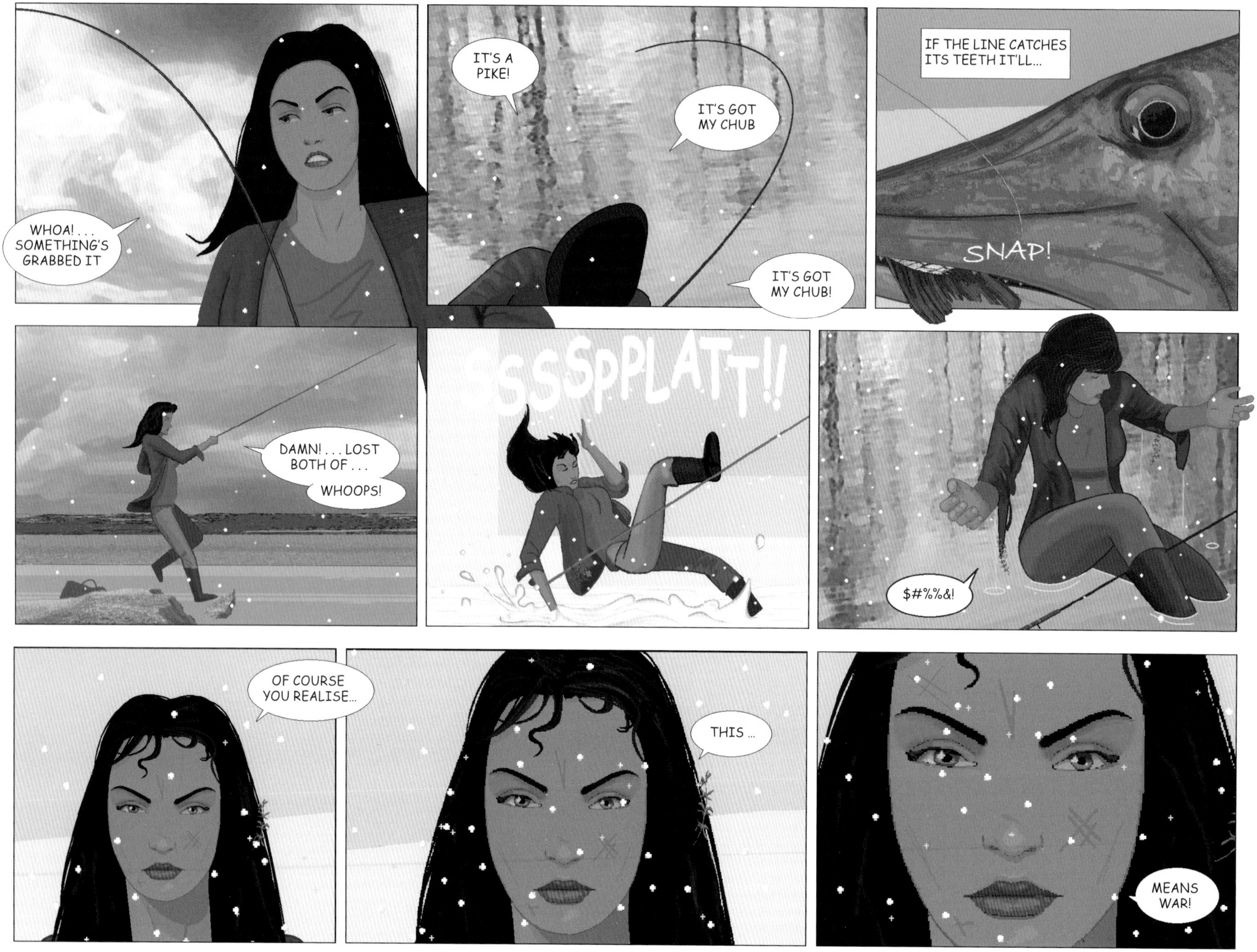
WHOA! . . . SOMETHING'S GRABBED IT
IT'S A PIKE!
IT'S GOT MY CHUB
IT'S GOT MY CHUB!
IF THE LINE CATCHES ITS TEETH IT'LL...
SNAP!
DAMN! . . . LOST BOTH OF . . .
WHOOPS!
SSSSPPLATTT!!
$#%%&!
OF COURSE YOU REALISE...
THIS ...
MEANS WAR!

PIKE AGAIN
TODAY

Merlin's
Braid

30.0lb
13.64kg
100m
0.24mm

18. Emma's revenge

You'll notice that as well as a Roach that's seen better days (above) is a spool marked 'Braid'. Emma's after Pike again today and is using this rather than Mono. Braid is very strong but at the same time very thin. It has a much lower diameter than Mono: a 40lb Braid might have a similar diameter to a 10lb Mono. Emma's using 30lb today which is fine for Pike. The way that Braid is made means that there's virtually no stretch in the line, so even gentle bites are obvious and the strike will set the hook instantly.

During the fight you'll feel every twist, turn, shake of the head and pull of the fish but this lack of stretch has consequences. If there's no give in the line, hook pull-outs are far more likely and a thin powerful braided line can bury itself into the spool when under pressure.

Both problems can be avoided by ensuring that the drag on the reel is not set too tightly: set it looser with Braid than with Mono.

Push line through eye, double back and push through again

Wrap 8 times around line then thread through loop

Moisten with saliva, pull tight then trim end

Braid is very limp and supple, has no memory and can be cast easily to great distance – it is however more expensive than Mono.

Using Braid will also require different knots (see left) and special scissors.

Now back to that unlucky Roach. We mentioned in a previous chapter that there are issues with using Coarse fish as deadbaits. Before using them you must check the fishery/venue rules. Nowadays some will only allow Sea fish to be used as deadbaits, others stipulate that you only use fish from the venue itself as deads, or that you

only use deadbaits that have been commercially frozen. These laws are intended to prevent anglers introducing disease-carrying fish from one water to another. Emma's using a Roach that she bought in a pack from her local tackle shop.

Emma's made up the rig herself using a single hook and a semi-barbless treble. The red bait flag helps to lock the barbed hook into the deadbait and also provides a splash of colour for the Pike to aim at (as does the bead). These rigs are often made up with a treble at the front instead of the single that Emma prefers.

You can secure the rig to the deadbait with baitfloss or an elastic band if you wish.

You can put a bend in the deadbait as you hook it up – this alters the

way it moves through the water and some anglers say this gives them an edge.

Sink and draw basically combines Lure fishing and deadbaiting, as the angler works the deadbait like a lure.

Emma's put a couple of large shot on the front of the trace and as she winds the deadbait in, it rises in the water. When she stops winding, the fish drops, falling and fluttering through the water, and the weights ensure it is head down. Imagine a badly-injured fish struggling to swim. Exhausted, it stops and falls, it tries again, struggling forward only to fall again. To a predator this is virtually irresistible. The Pike doesn't want to waste effort and energy chasing a healthy fish around, it wants an easy meal, an instant kill.

If the angler does his job, the wobbled deadbait will offer the Pike this easy meal.

But there's more to it than this. I remember fishing with a friend who'd spotted a Pike lying alongside a weedbed. He kept putting his lure in front of the fish, which consistently ignored it. Undeterred he kept casting to the Pike and winding the lure in just past its nose. On about the tenth cast the Pike suddenly lost it and lurched forward, grabbing the lure and shaking its head like a dog with a rat.

Usually Pike will strike out of hunger but not always – sometimes it's territorial instinct and sometimes just sheer belligerence.

The angler can do their bit. As with Lure fishing, think about the way that you retrieve the deadbait. A sharp flick of the rod tip before you let the bait drop and varying the speed of the retrieve can often make all the difference.

This method probably works best in clear water with a slow retrieve. Use the depth of the water as well and don't be afraid of leaving the bait on the bottom for a few minutes now and again before you retrieve.

When working an artificial, you must keep it moving for it to work. With a wobbled deadbait, if it's lying on the bottom, it's still a deadbait so any Pike picking it up or touching it won't feel anything strange. This can't be said of a Lure.

A wobbled deadbait that's been left on the bottom for a minute or two can often induce a strike when moved, as waiting Pike will often hit the bait if it thinks it's getting away.

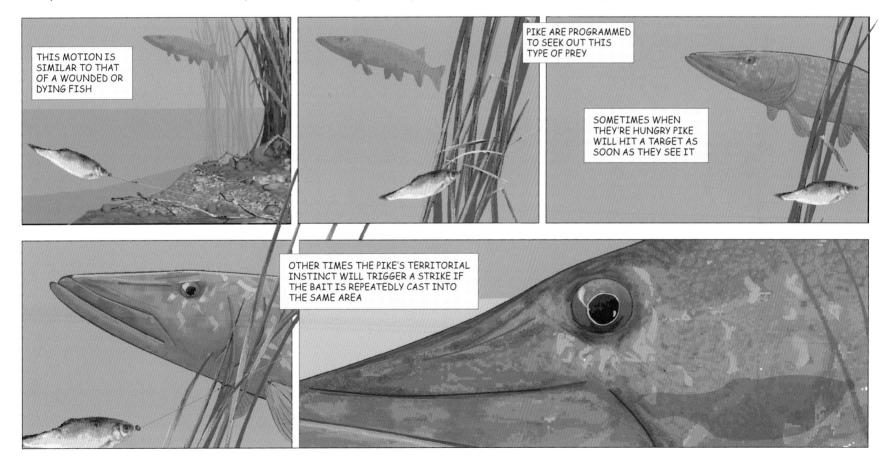

THIS MOTION IS SIMILAR TO THAT OF A WOUNDED OR DYING FISH

PIKE ARE PROGRAMMED TO SEEK OUT THIS TYPE OF PREY

SOMETIMES WHEN THEY'RE HUNGRY PIKE WILL HIT A TARGET AS SOON AS THEY SEE IT

OTHER TIMES THE PIKE'S TERRITORIAL INSTINCT WILL TRIGGER A STRIKE IF THE BAIT IS REPEATEDLY CAST INTO THE SAME AREA

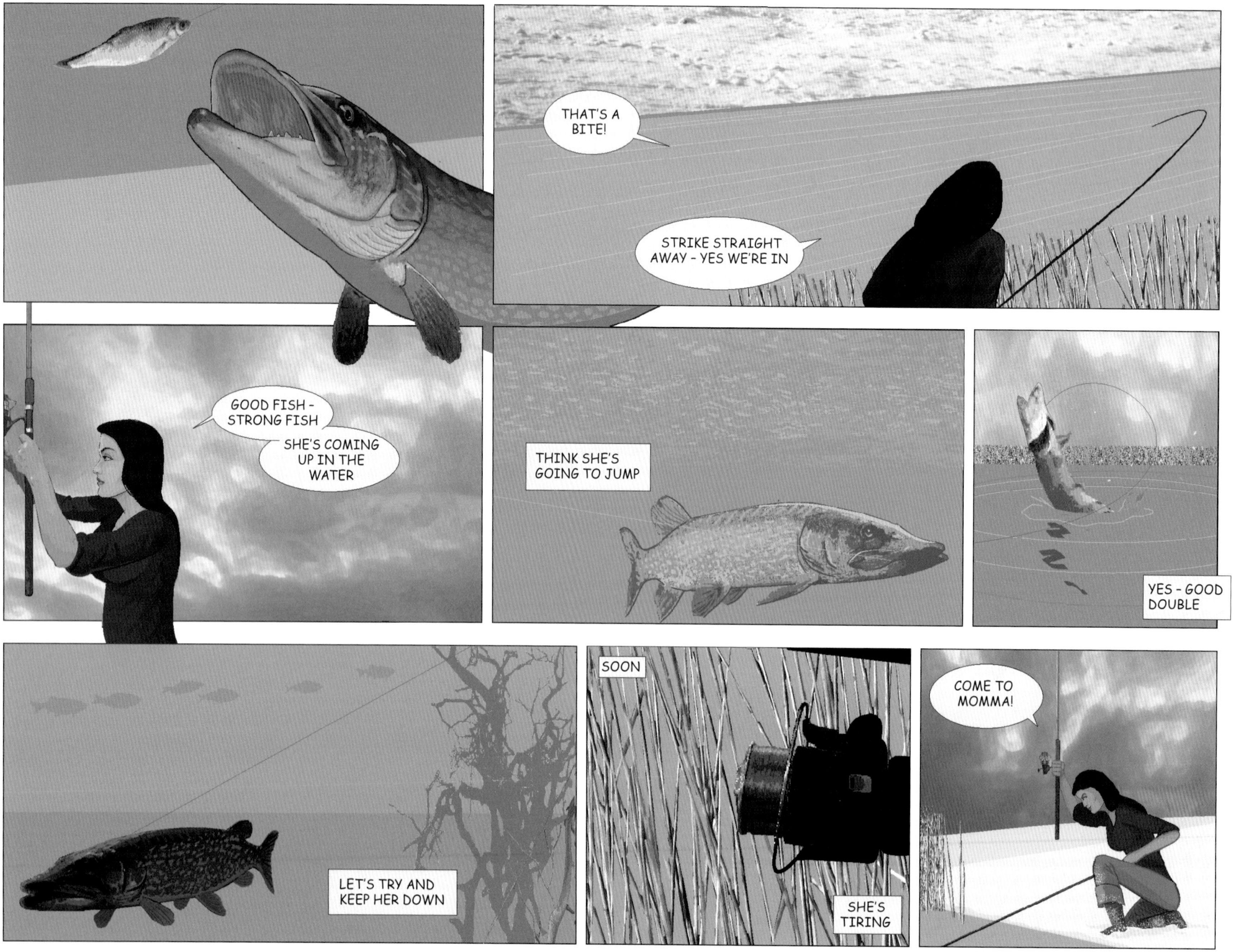
THAT'S A BITE!
STRIKE STRAIGHT AWAY - YES WE'RE IN
GOOD FISH - STRONG FISH
SHE'S COMING UP IN THE WATER
THINK SHE'S GOING TO JUMP
YES - GOOD DOUBLE
LET'S TRY AND KEEP HER DOWN
SOON
SHE'S TIRING
COME TO MOMMA!

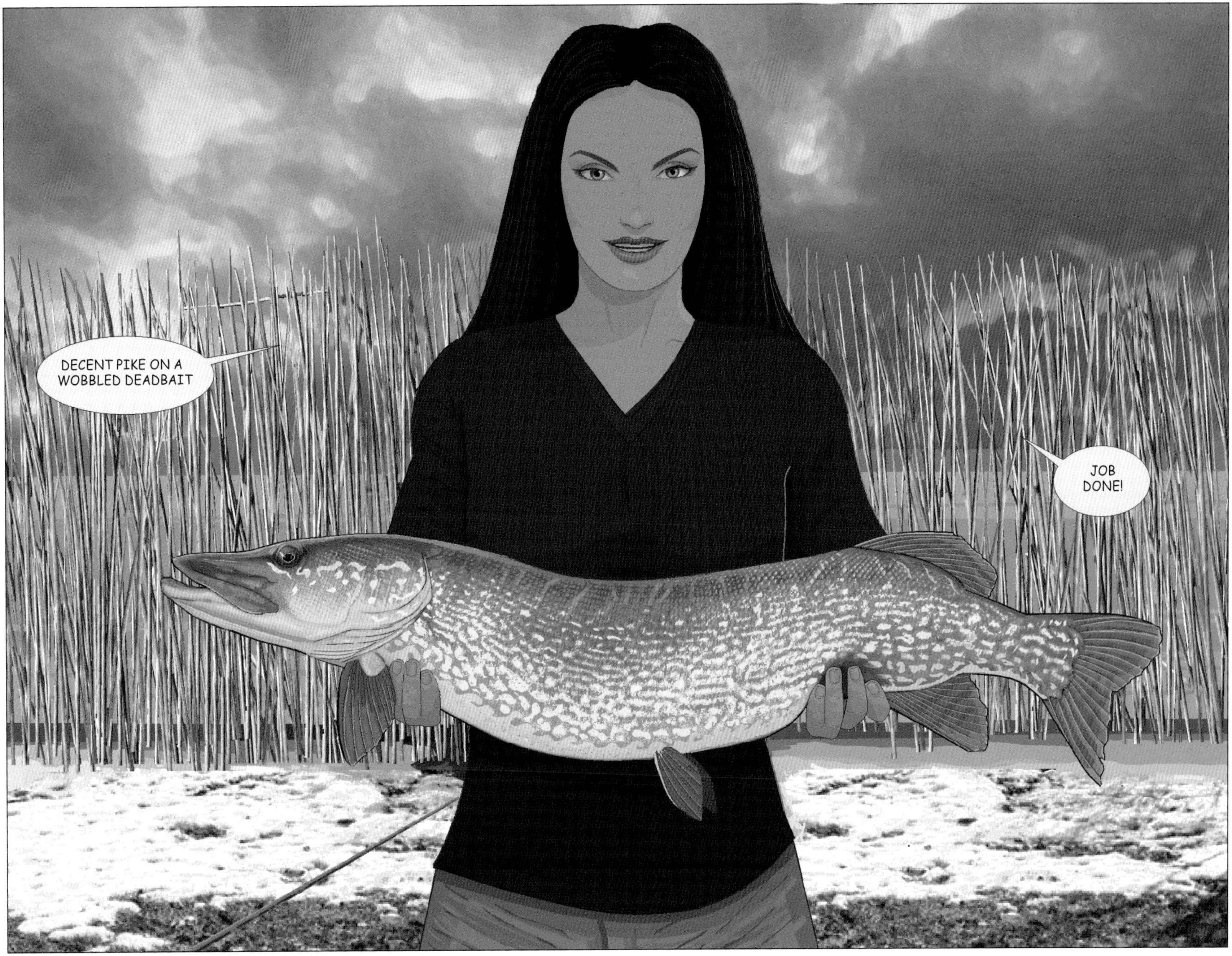
DECENT PIKE ON A WOBBLED DEADBAIT
JOB DONE!

TOMORROW WE'RE SPECIMEN HUNTING AND BELIEVE ME ...

I'VE SAVED THE BEST TILL LAST!

1lb 4oz River Wye 1959

19. Spikes and Stripes

There are many disciplines in Coarse fishing. Some anglers concentrate on single species such as Carp, others fish matches and many specialise in Specimen hunting. Specimen hunting involves searching for the big fish of one or more species.

Emma's caught several large fish in this book: a double-figure Pike, several large Carp and that Catfish but a large fish is not necessarily a Specimen.

On the wall of her study is a Dace she found in an antique shop. The fish is a little over a pound, a tiny fish compared to a twenty pound Carp but that Carp is less than a third of the British record, whilst the Dace is barely an ounce or two under.

So are Specimens in reach of a novice angler on a budget? Well, it depends on the species. In the case of Carp, probably not. The growth of Carp fisheries has impacted on other species and Bream and Tench have grown huge along-side Carp and the way that many Commercial fisheries are set up has greatly benefited at least two other species – Roach and Perch.

As there aren't usually Pike present in Commercials, the Perch become top predators and are rarely targeted by anglers.

The best time of year to hunt these stunning creatures (autumn-early Spring) is often when the fishery is at its quietest.

Angling legend Richard Walker described the Perch as the biggest fish of all. A big Perch on the bank really has to be seen to be believed.

The fish are bold, brassy and aggressively beautiful, the markings and colouration unlike anything else. The mouth is huge, the eyes are bright and the whole effect is breathtaking. For me they are without doubt the most beautiful of all Coarse fish. A big Perch on the bank is all anger and bristling defiance, once seen, never forgotten.

And big Perch nowadays are a real possibility. Do a little research, talk to other anglers, ask at your local tackle shop, and you could find yourself attached to one of the most exciting creatures than an angler can encounter.

Emma's fishing in winter. It's not been that cold and the weedbeds will provide these sharp-eyed predators with the cover they love.

Emma's not using fish as bait (it's not allowed on this fishery) but worm, prawns and maggots have all provided many Perch for her in the past. A favourite technique with many who fish for Perch is to feed maggots then fish worm over the top. The maggots attract small silver fish and large Perch will follow them. A worm (particularly if it's moved regularly) will rarely be ignored if there's Perch about.

The key to rigging up for them is to avoid resistance. If Perch feel any when they pick up a bait, they'll drop it straightaway.

Emma's banded a small weighted Waggler (a float fixed top and bottom will offer less resistance as it slides under) and placed a No. 1 shot directly under it.

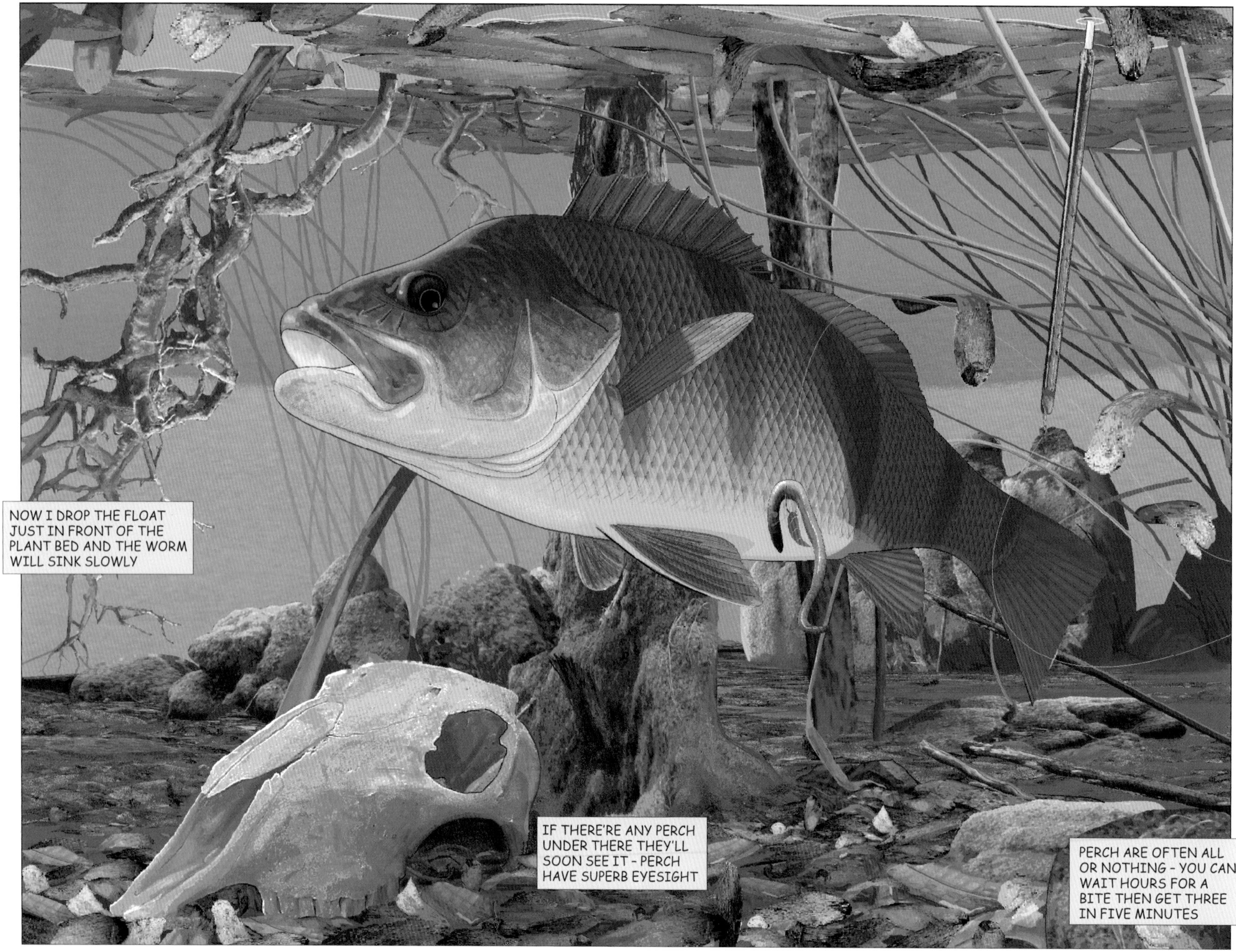
NOW I DROP THE FLOAT JUST IN FRONT OF THE PLANT BED AND THE WORM WILL SINK SLOWLY
IF THERE'RE ANY PERCH UNDER THERE THEY'LL SOON SEE IT - PERCH HAVE SUPERB EYESIGHT
PERCH ARE OFTEN ALL OR NOTHING - YOU CAN WAIT HOURS FOR A BITE THEN GET THREE IN FIVE MINUTES

Only the tip shows on the surface, just enough for Emma to see (she'll be mainly fishing the margins). This small amount of float above the surface offers minimum resistance to a taking fish. Usually if Perch are around you won't have long to wait (provided they're in the mood).

Emma will fish one weedbed then move on to another. It pays to raise and drop the rod every five minutes or so – just to move the bait (this often induces a bite). It can pay to bring the bait in a few turns at a time, fish one spot then instead of just winding in, bring it in a few feet then leave it.

Now we mentioned the stunning colours of the Perch. The greens and reds that you can see in the fish that Emma's holding will show you what the fish should look like but the one drawback with these huge Perch

from Commercials is that they're rarely coloured like this.

Look at the colour of the fish in the top right panel of this page. Blues and greys for the greens; pinks and purples instead of reds. A large Commercial Perch is more likely to look like this than the ideal (no problems with their attitude though). Some say this is down to the muddy waters of Commercial Carp ponds but the muddy waters of our local canal has produced hundreds of perfectly coloured mini monsters, so I doubt this is the reason.

With Aquarium fish, to get the best out of their colour it's necessary to get stocking levels and water chemistry spot on. Maybe conditions in modern Commercials are just a little too artificial, not that any of this matters when you slide your landing net under the fish of a lifetime.

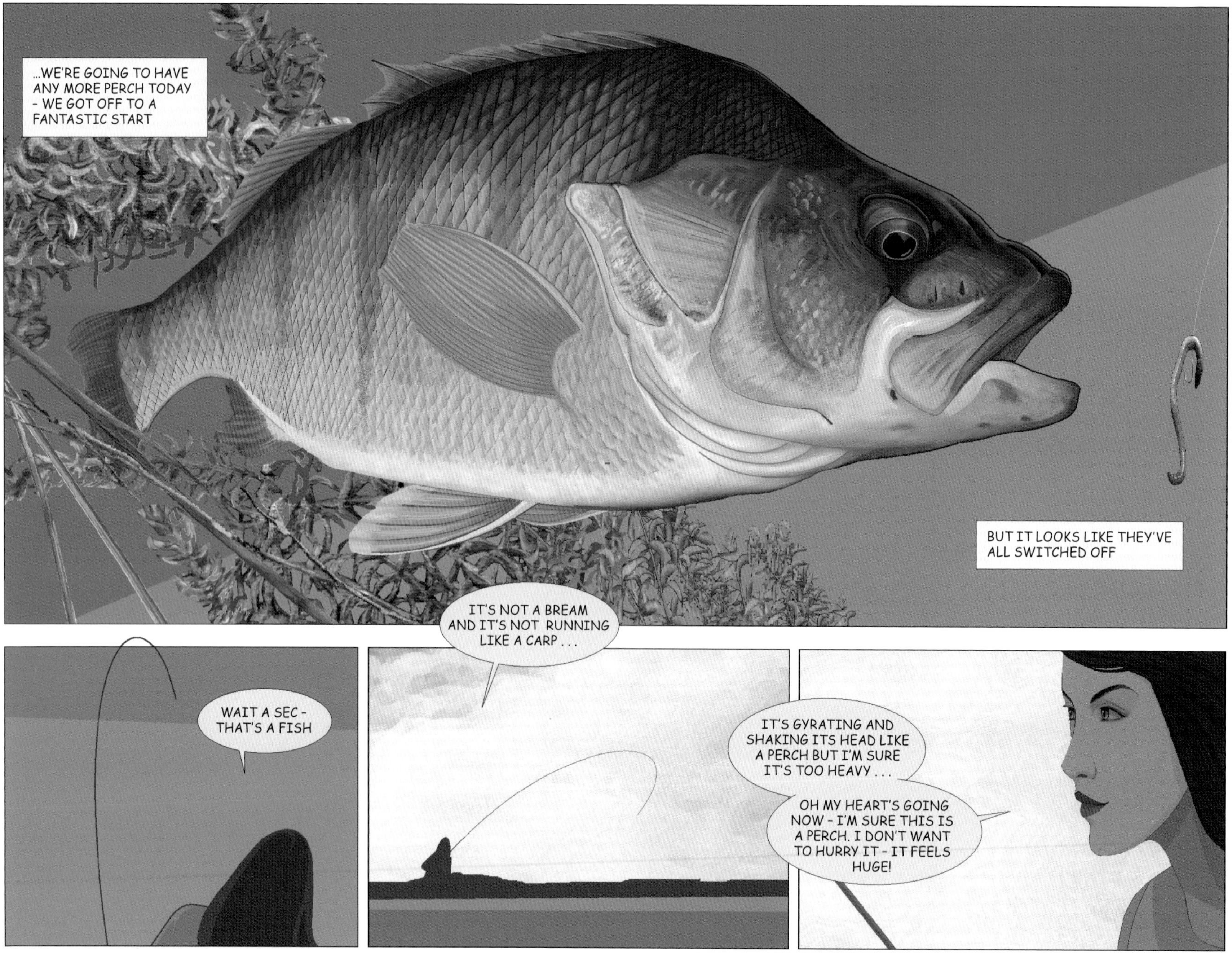
...WE'RE GOING TO HAVE ANY MORE PERCH TODAY - WE GOT OFF TO A FANTASTIC START
BUT IT LOOKS LIKE THEY'VE ALL SWITCHED OFF
WAIT A SEC - THAT'S A FISH
IT'S NOT A BREAM AND IT'S NOT RUNNING LIKE A CARP . . .
IT'S GYRATING AND SHAKING ITS HEAD LIKE A PERCH BUT I'M SURE IT'S TOO HEAVY . . .
OH MY HEART'S GOING NOW - I'M SURE THIS IS A PERCH. I DON'T WANT TO HURRY IT - IT FEELS HUGE!

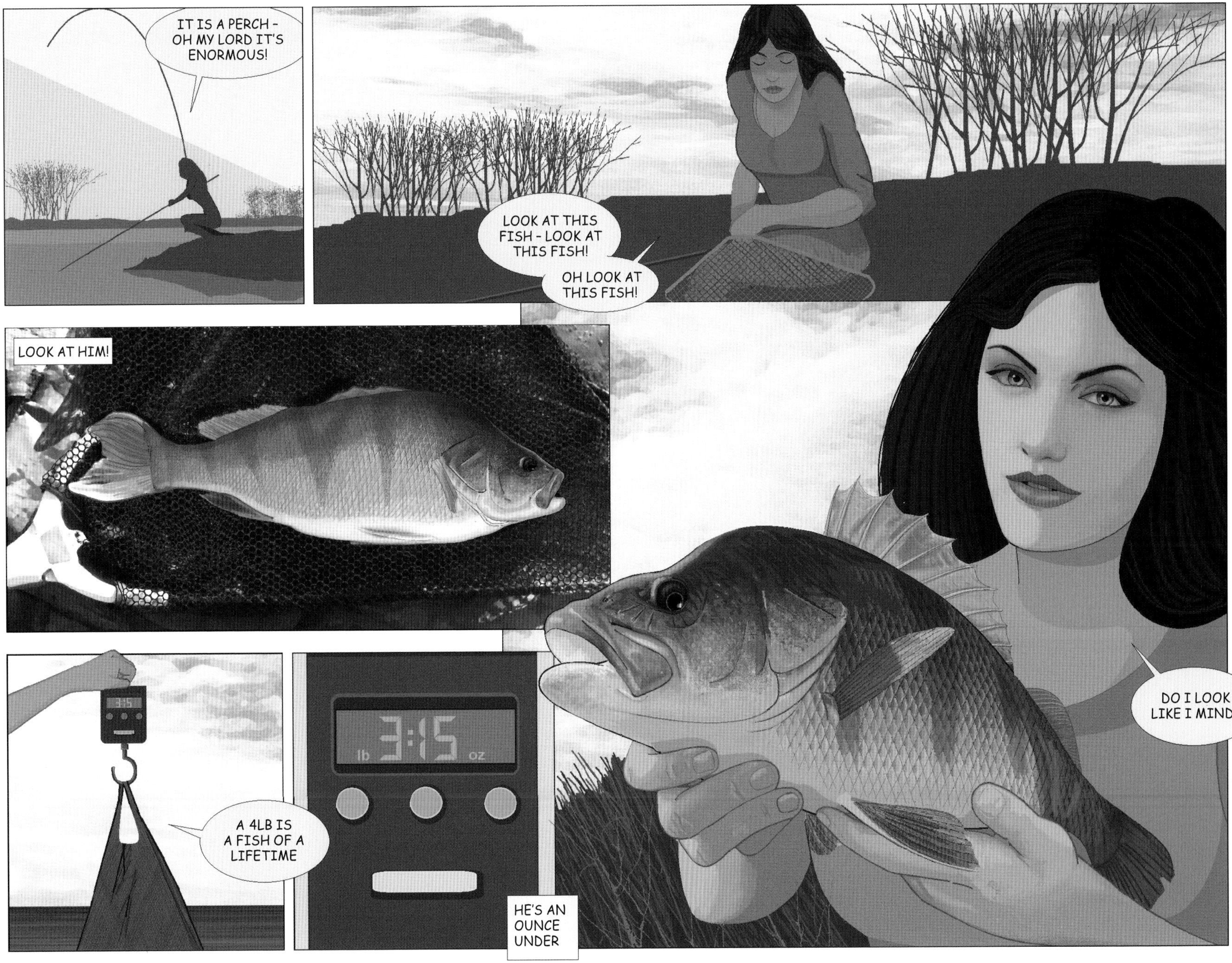
IT IS A PERCH - OH MY LORD IT'S ENORMOUS!
LOOK AT THIS FISH - LOOK AT THIS FISH!
OH LOOK AT THIS FISH!
LOOK AT HIM!
DO I LOOK LIKE I MIND?
A 4LB IS A FISH OF A LIFETIME
3:15
lb
oz
HE'S AN OUNCE UNDER

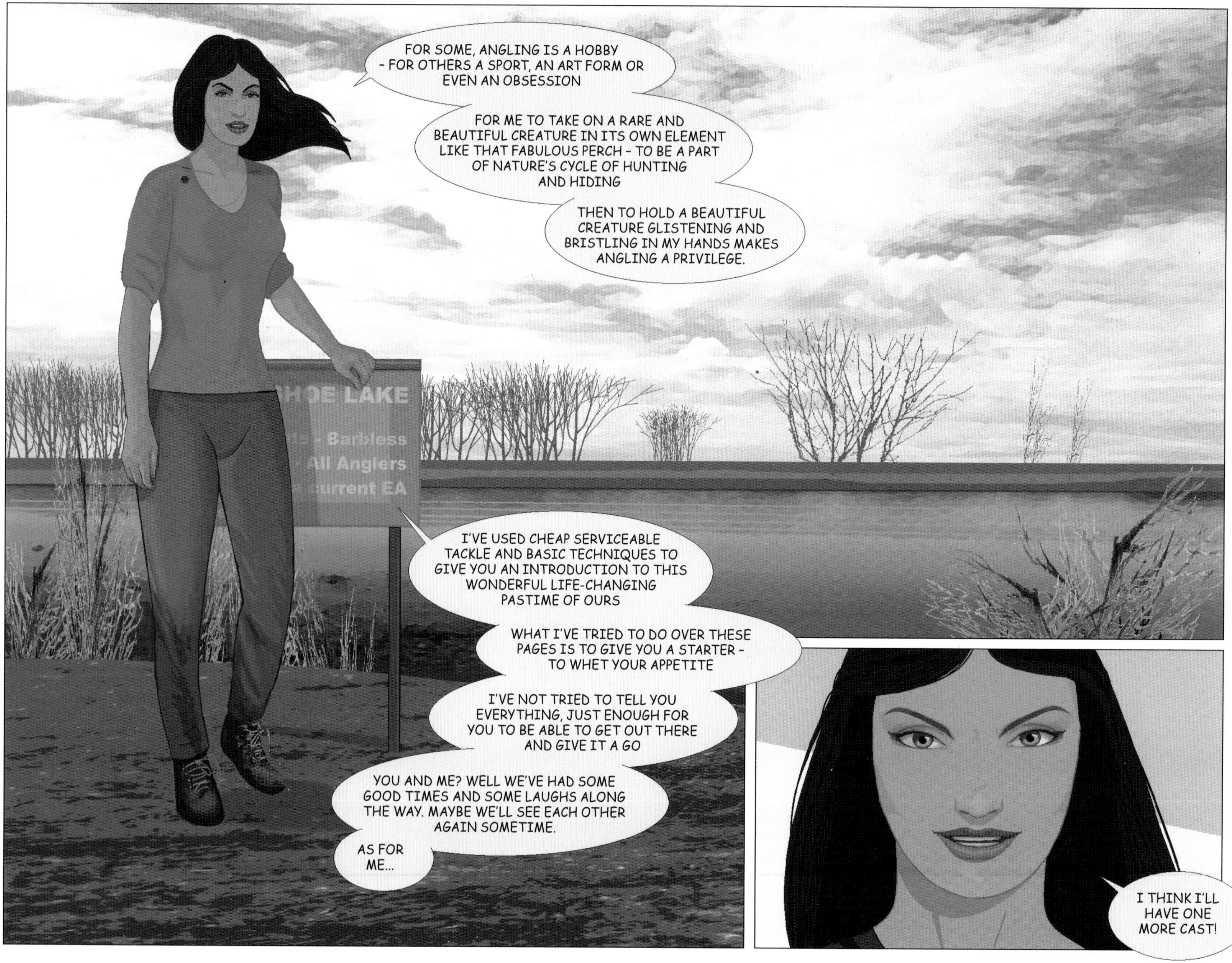
FOR SOME, ANGLING IS A HOBBY - FOR OTHERS A SPORT, AN ART FORM OR EVEN AN OBSESSION
FOR ME TO TAKE ON A RARE AND BEAUTIFUL CREATURE IN ITS OWN ELEMENT LIKE THAT FABULOUS PERCH - TO BE A PART OF NATURE'S CYCLE OF HUNTING AND HIDING
THEN TO HOLD A BEAUTIFUL CREATURE GLISTENING AND BRISTLING IN MY HANDS MAKES ANGLING A PRIVILEGE.
Barbless
All Anglers
I'VE USED CHEAP SERVICEABLE TACKLE AND BASIC TECHNIQUES TO GIVE YOU AN INTRODUCTION TO THIS WONDERFUL LIFE-CHANGING PASTIME OF OURS
WHAT I'VE TRIED TO DO OVER THESE PAGES IS TO GIVE YOU A STARTER - TO WHET YOUR APPETITE
I'VE NOT TRIED TO TELL YOU EVERYTHING, JUST ENOUGH FOR YOU TO BE ABLE TO GET OUT THERE AND GIVE IT A GO
YOU AND ME? WELL WE'VE HAD SOME GOOD TIMES AND SOME LAUGHS ALONG THE WAY. MAYBE WE'LL SEE EACH OTHER AGAIN SOMETIME.
AS FOR ME...
I THINK I'LL HAVE ONE MORE CAST!